Ge

the
Complete
Guide *to their*
Music

OMNIBUS PRESS
London / New York / Paris /
Sydney / Copenhagen
Berlin / Madrid / Tokyo

Chris Welch

Book and cover designed by Chloë Alexander
Picture research by Sarah Bacon

Cover image courtesy of Corbis

ISBN: 1.84449.868.9
Order No: OP50875

Exclusive Distributors
Music Sales Limited,
8/9 Frith Street,
London W1D 3JB, UK.

Music Sales Corporation,
257 Park Avenue South,
New York, NY 10010, USA.

Macmillan Distribution Services,
53 Park West Drive,
Derrimut, Vic 3030,
Australia.

To the Music Trade only
Music Sales Limited,
8/9 Frith Street,
London W1D 3JB, UK.

Every effort has been made to trace the copyright holders
of the photographs in this book but one or two were
unreachable. We would be grateful if the photographers
concerned would contact us.

Printed in Great Britain by Mackays of Chatham plc,
Chatham Kent

A catalogue record for this book is available from the
British Library.

Visit Omnibus Press on the web at
www.omnibuspress.com

Contents

INTRODUCTION

GENESIS ARE UNIQUE AMONG CLASSIC BRITISH ROCK BANDS IN HAVING achieved an impressive output of consistently innovative albums. For a quarter of a century, from 1969 to 1997, their recorded work has provided a kind of Bayeux Tapestry of musical progress, pricked and stitched by occasional battles, alarums and excursions.

There have been longer surviving bands: The Rolling Stones, for example, make Genesis look like stripling newcomers. But until 1994's *Voodoo Lounge* many critics complained the Stones hadn't made a decent album in years. Genesis, however, despite a few glitches en route, have always moved ahead, each work displaying some improvement, or at least a cluster of new ideas.

And it hasn't all been a dull, safe pedestrian process either. Just when it was thought the band might have reached a dead end, or passed their sell-by date, they have confounded the critics, revitalised their music and gained their most resounding hits. The great Genesis Come Back had become a regular occurrence, until they finally decided to call a halt in 2000, after *Calling All Stations* (1997). This proved to be their final studio album, made in the wake of Phil Collins' departure with new singer Ray Wilson.

Phil Collins' role had been pivotal to the commercial success of what had previously been described as an 'art rock' band. It was during the drummer-turned-singer's watch that Genesis underwent a transformation of fortunes. After Peter Gabriel, their prominent lead singer, quit the band in May, 1975, many wondered how the band divested of its theatrical front man (prone to wearing masks, costumes and disguises on stage), would fare without him. They fared very well. Far from slumping into a slough of despond, Genesis evolved into a mega rock stadium attraction.

Genesis then went on to survive the onslaught of punk rock, and became one of the few Seventies' bands to prosper and win new audiences in the Eighties. They underwent many splits and changes of direction along the way. But in the process they created a kind of Rock University whose most distinguished 'old boys', Phil Collins and Peter Gabriel, began to dominate the music industry, unleashing a veritable cascade of hit solo albums and singles. Their colleagues – Steve Hackett, Tony Banks and Mike Rutherford – have also enjoyed their own levels of success, to the point where Genesis-related product at times swamped international charts in the teeth of competition from many high profile contemporary artists.

The graduates of the Genesis school have certainly done their homework. Their first album *From Genesis To Revelation* (1969), saw the band set out its wares and determine its future policy. Arrangements, soundscapes, unusual lyrics, imaginative use of a range of instruments and dramatic, memorable themes would be at the heart of their music and presentation from the outset.

While Genesis was first perceived as a neo-classical 'albums band' there was no lack of humour in their work and they were adept at creating three-minute classic hits. Certainly, they were celebrated for dramatised, extended works like 'The Knife', 'The Musical Box', 'The Return Of the Giant Hogweed', 'Watcher Of The Skies' and 'Supper's Ready' which illuminated a trio of early albums, *Trespass*, *Nursery Cryme* and *Foxtrot*.
However, the band was always capable of editing its work, producing short songs that reflected an affinity with pop.

Both Peter Gabriel and Phil Collins grew up listening to Tamla Motown and were unabashed fans of The Who and The Beatles. In the midst of creating orchestrated epics, rich in keyboard and guitar solos, many effective short form Genesis ditties worked their way into the singles charts. From 'I Know What I Like' in 1974 through to 'Mama', 'Invisible Touch' and 'I Can't Dance' in 1992, Genesis unleashed a steady flow of memorable hits.

They were greatly assisted by the advent of promo videos in the Eighties, as they modernised and updated their sound and image from such albums as *Duke* and *Abacab* onwards.

Genesis' recording career has been a sort of balancing act, involving their own needs as writers and performers, the skills of various producers, new technological developments and dictates of changing public taste.

Genesis began as unknown schoolboys, encouraged by producer Jonathan King to tackle a Biblical theme for their first album. When this failed to set the world ablaze, they resolved to develop their own ideas, bringing in new musicians, until they settled on the line up of Peter Gabriel (vocals, flute), Mike Rutherford (guitars, basses), Tony Banks (keyboards), Steve Hackett (guitars) and Phil Collins (drums and vocals).

An entertaining stage act won them a dedicated 'underground' following, they mixed theatrical concepts with elements of classical and rock music.

Their early albums, reflecting their shows, were packed with brilliant images and themes. Next came the ambitious double set *The Lamb Lies Down On Broadway*. It meant so much to Peter Gabriel, who took responsibility for the concept, that he quit the band when it caused more controversy both within and without the group than he could bear.

After this watershed album, Genesis moved into a period of more mellow and introspective works like *A Trick Of The Tail*, *Wind And Wuthering* and *...And Then There Were Three* with drummer Phil now assuming the role of lead singer. The band was whittled away to a three-piece, following the departure of Steve Hackett in 1978. Banks, Rutherford and Collins held the Genesis banner aloft in the studio, while the touring band took in drummers Bill Bruford and Chester Thompson and guitarist Daryl Stuermer. These musicians would be featured only on the band's 'live' albums, but the studio albums would continue to be devised by the core members in conjunction with producers David Hentschel, Hugh Padgham and Nick Davis.

The early Eighties saw Genesis abandon its overtly 'progressive rock' stance, as they brought in brass players and and drum machines. There was less scope for the rhapsodic piano and organ solos that had been such a feature of their past work. However, with a powerful new drum sound, and Collins' dominating vocal presence, the tightly produced Genesis records of the techno decade had enormous impact.

On latter day albums *Genesis*, *Invisible Touch* and *We Can't Dance*, the band skilfully blended past experience in a gush of creativity, often improvising on the spot such extraordinary works as the hypnotic 'Mama'.

Some die-hard fans mourned the passing of 'the old Genesis' yet the grand procession of albums shows they never stopped experimenting and were always trying to produce the ultimate Genesis album. After all – that's why they called it 'progressive rock'.

Given the seismic changes in the music industry, even since the band's last studio album *Calling All Stations*, it is remarkable that interest in Genesis remains stronger than ever. Although the band stopped touring and the members concentrated on their solo careers, there has been an impressive programme of re-issues paying tribute to their remarkable legacy. The band's original allbums have been re-issued on re-mastered CDs and special collections released, including *Archive 1967-75*, a 4 CD box-set (1998), *Turn It On Again: The Hits* (1999) *Archive Volume 2 1976-1992* triple set (2000) and the *Platinum Collection* (2004). A new version of *The Lamb Lies Down On Broadway*, a 5.1 remix by producer

Nick Davis, was scheduled for release in May 2005.

Phil Collins stated in December 2004 that after a long and fruitful career he now wanted to spend more time with his family. As for a Genesis reunion he added: "We still get on great. There's no reason why we can't see each other and remain friends. There's no reason why we shouldn't write songs together. But a Genesis tour is out of the question."

It would be fascinating to see all of the past participants re-united for one final team effort, the one that Mike Rutherford has described as the ULTIMATE Genesis album. Perhaps, reverting to the Bible once more for inspiration, they could call it... *Genesis: The Last Supper.*

Chris Welch
London, England 2005

From Genesis
To Revelation

Original UK issue: Decca SKL 4990, released March 1969;
re-issued as *Roots* in 1976 with additional tracks.
Re-issued again as *Where The Sour Turns To Sweet* on Rock Machine
MACHM 4 (1986); CD as *From Genesis To Revelation* on Razor MACHK 11
(1988); CD *From Genesis To Revelation* on Music Club MCCD 132 (1993);
CD *From Genesis To Revelation* Deluxe 2 CD Edition
on Edsel MEDCD 721 (2005)

DIE HARD ROCK FANS USUALLY CLAIM THAT "THE FIRST TWO ALBUMS ARE the best", when discussing the works of their favourite bands. Certainly Zeppelin-ites had cause to praise the dynamic debut made by Plant, Page & Co. when *Led Zeppelin* was released in 1969. It caused a sensation and launched the band on its extraordinary career.

The same year another budding supergroup unleashed their first album. Alas it proved possibly the most inauspicious debut in the annals of rock and was doomed to obscurity. Fortunately Genesis survived and learned to profit by their mistakes.

Genesis could not be blamed if *From Genesis To Revelation* wasn't a huge success. Here was an unknown, inexperienced bunch of schoolboys, attempting to launch themselves with a remarkably ambitious recording project. Their theme was the creation of the world, as told in *The Bible* and the subsequent evolution of Mankind. It was a bit like a local film club attempting to re-make *Ben Hur* for their first movie project. It's commercial failure almost broke up the group and the album remained an unmentionable topic for many years. Few fans were even aware of its existence when the band achieved success in the early Seventies.

Despite its faults, the album did have considerable artistic merit. It gave an indication of Peter Gabriel's unique vocal qualities, the imaginative scope of his lyric writing and the musical capabilities of Tony Banks, whose superb piano playing was well to the fore. It is possible to hear in these primitive, tentative first steps, the most important aspects of a style they would develop over the coming years.

The seeds of the album were sown in 1967 when a band of Charterhouse public schoolboys sent a demo tape to Jonathan King at Decca Records. Jonathan was an 'old boy' from the school, but didn't actually know the lads, then so eager to break into the music business. Nevertheless he was impressed by the tape, the product of two groups, one called The Garden Wall and the other The Anon, now combined into a new outfit called – The New Anon.

The band members included Peter Gabriel, and Tony Banks, with Anthony Phillips (guitar), Chris Stewart (drums), and Mike Rutherford (bass). Chris was later replaced by John Silver. They were all still at school and between 15 and 17 years old , when they were signed to Decca for a one year record contract. Jonathan King, who had written and sung a Top 20 hit, 'Everyone's Gone To The Moon', when he was still a Cambridge undergraduate, now had his own publishing company Jonjo Music Ltd and was looking for talent to develop.

He signed them to his company and gave them the princely sum of £40 for four songs and began recording them at London's Regent Sound. He wasn't overly impressed by their first demos, until Banks and Gabriel came up with a song they thought would have more pop appeal. It was a Bee Gees-style effort called 'The Silent Sun', coupled with 'That's Me' on the B side. It was released on Decca in February 1968, but their début single failed to get into the charts. The next single 'A Winter's Tale' was also a flop.

King retained his faith in their potential and during August the band was invited to record an album. They had just recruited new drummer, John Silver, and they had done hardly any live gigs, but they had done a lot of rehearsing. Jonathan suggested their kind of introspective, thoughtful material might best be suited to a concept album, and came up with the idea of doing *From Genesis To Revelation*.

The band wrote the material and rehearsed it during the school holidays at John Silver's home in the country, then returned to London to record the whole lot at Regent Sound in one day. They were quite nervous and according to legend Peter Gabriel had to keep taking cold showers to help him hit the high notes. Although Tony Banks' piano was strong and authoritative, the rhythm section was fairly weak and to fill out the sound and give the music an appropriately Biblical splendour, Jonathan added strings arranged by musical director Arthur Greenslade. It was an idea that had been deemed successful on 'A Silent Sun', but the band was unhappy about the rather syrupy strings which took up the whole of one stereo channel, while they were confined to the other.

It was released in March, 1969 to lukewarm reviews and without any radio plays, it sank without trace. Its black cover with gold lettering didn't help sales, as some stores placed it in their religious record racks.

The experience virtually ended the band's relationship with Jonathan King. They told him they had broken up, and retreated back to the country to think about their future. At least King had given them one lasting legacy of their time together – the band's new name – Genesis.

Recalls Tony Banks: "We did the whole album in a day. We got into the studio at 9am and worked right through until midnight the following day with Jonathan King producing. We were very young and it was an amateur sort of approach, but there are a couple of good songs and I think the album was quite good. It's been endlessly repackaged since, but it sold nothing at the time."

The album sold just 650 copies and after its failure Banks went to Sussex University to begin a physics course, before music lured him back to the group. "When we made the album we had never really played live. It was based on piano and acoustic guitar with other things over dubbed. Then they put some strings and brass arrangements on, which we had a hand in writing. It all became a bit lighter than was originally intended. My favourite track was 'In The Wilderness'. Peter's voice sounded really good on it. We were just out of school and it was fun for us. To be given a chance to make an album was amazing. Jonathan selected the tracks but we had a whole stack more. I still have the tapes at home of all sorts of songs that never made it onto that album, some of which are quite good.

"The pastoral songs worked all right, but the more aggressive songs didn't really come across. Jonathan was very good for the band in the early days. If it hadn't been for him, we wouldn't have got going."

Mike Rutherford recalled: "The album was dissatisfying artistically because the songs didn't come out as we wanted them to. But it gave us a glimpse of what we could do."

Says Jonathan King: "It was one of the great underrated albums. It was fairly revolutionary thinking from a bunch of young people. The album was ahead of its time."

From Genesis To Revelation has been re-issued many times, usually with the first two singles, 'The Silent Sun' and 'A Winter's Tale', and their B sides included as bonus tracks.

In 2005 a Deluxe 2-CD Edition of the album was issued. It has a facsimile of the original 1969 Decca LP cover and with a slipcase package featuring, for the first time since the vinyl release, Peter Gabriel's sleevenotes with lyrics and drawings. Disc 1 contained the original 13 song album and Disc 2 comprised four non-album single sides and a further nine items of demos, single A and B sides and rough mixes from 1967 and 1968 arranged chronologically.

Edsel CD Disc One

WHERE THE SOUR TURNS TO SWEET

ARTHUR Greenslade's strings tend to get in the way of an otherwise powerful song, full of quirky humour. Gabriel makes early use of a favourite device; emphasising a single word to extract full meaning, as he sings: 'Come and join us NOW!' There are some jazzy, echoing 'finger pops' behind Banks' firm piano chords to give a swing feel. The song has great charm, but the fade out ending is carelessly inconclusive. This was the last of their Decca single releases and it also failed to chart.

IN THE BEGINNING

STRANGE whining noises, probably Regent Sound's hired synthesiser, are used – presumably to symbolise the creation of the universe. This leads on to a pushing, thrusting vocal, with the sort of menacing urgency that was to become the hallmark of the classic Genesis style. It was the sort of thing Phil Collins would exploit much later in both his and the band's career. Peter furiously declaims key phrases in stabbing tones, as the musical story of creation and Man's evolution unfolds.

You have to admire their boldness in coping with such a vast subject, one few established bands would have attempted, let alone a bunch of novices.

FIRESIDE SONG

PETER Gabriel may have been edgy during the recording of this first album but his vocals here are quite beautiful. He sings in a very English manner, "Once upon a time there was confusion, disappointment, fear and disillusion." Burdened by the perils of the world, singing a warning hymn of peace. His phrases leap out from the somewhat mundane melody and acoustic guitar accompaniment: "The trees defied the world and shook their leaves."

THE SERPENT

THE DRAMATIC use of silence is instructive here, showing that Genesis knew all about the value of dynamics quite early on in their evolution. The album may have been ostensibly about the creation of the world, but it was really about the creation of a new group, taking its first tentative steps in a musical direction they were determined to pursue. There is more evidence of ideas that would recur in later works, notably *The Lamb Lies Down On Broadway*. Sings Gabriel: "Creator made the serpent wise, evil in his tempting eyes." The lead guitar riff is quite strong, building up a head of steam as Peter chants: "Beware the future!"

AM I VERY WRONG?

FRENCH horn and piano are blended with what sounds like a school choir at an end of term concert. It's melodic, but flimsy material and its hardly surprising that the album could not command any attention during an era dominated by heavy rock. Gabriel sings in a straightforward fashion some quite difficult 'wordy' lyrics.

IN THE WILDERNESS

BY THE close of side one of the vinyl album, the patience of the most dedicated student of the Biblical theory of creation must have found their patience wearing thin and enthusiasm flagging. But those who persevered were rewarded by hearing one of the more successful pieces. Gabriel chants, "Music, all I hear is music," with a spirit that recalls some of the wilder moments of The Who on *Tommy*. A more sombre note is sounded by Tony Banks playing a reprise of the theme in the final bars.

THE CONQUEROR

STRANGELY enough, there are more hints of The Who as Peter sings: "Justice day is coming as The Conqueror is on his way," but in truth the vocals sound a bit lost and flat. The whole piece is rendered duller than intended by the use of long drawn out backing notes. The omnipresent strings drag the beat, even though the drummer does his best to pep things up. Potentially a good piece, like so much of the material, it gets bogged down. A distant guitar, not quite in tune, gets lost in the mix.

IN HIDING

PERFORMED in 3/4 waltz time, this gentle concoction relies on Peter's angelic vocals for its effect. Sounding nervous, but charming, he warbles: "I have a mind of my own!" and adds curiously enough: "I will take off my clothes that I wear on my face."

ONE DAY

PETER sings over a Beatles' style trumpet backing on the final version of a fast and snappy song, where once again the piano proves the strongest musical factor. The final sustained chord has echoes of The Beatles 'A Day In The Life'. The 1968 rough mix of this song featured on the *Archive* box set and the Edsel 2005 re-issue is actually quite appealing and is certainly more atmospheric. Clearly, attempts to make the band's early material more commercial only served to detract from their original intentions.

WINDOW

A HONKY tonk piano is used here, doubtless with tin tacks pressed into the hammers to get that riveting sound. Lyrically and vocally it's a flat, one-dimensional performance, probably due to the need to record virtually everything in one day. Peter sounds like he's reading the lyrics off scraps of paper in his vocal booth.

IN LIMBO

S TRONGER brass playing enlivens this piece with stabbing 'flares' behind a chanted cry of 'Take me away!' Try as they might, a sense of ennui creeps into even the strongest pieces, and this particular item sounds very much like a rehearsal. It is in dire need of firm drums and less clutter, all priorities that would only receive attention when the band changed and enlarged its personnel.

SILENT SUN

A DRAMATIC piano introduction sets up the mood for Peter Gabriel's vocals on a subtle, gently swelling ballad, blessed with a strong hook line. It has a strong melody backed by sympathetic strings, but sounds strongly influenced by The Bee Gees. The band's plan here was to impress producer Jonathan King. However, such material would seem strange to latter day Genesis fans when the Decca material was re-issued long after the original release had been forgotten. There were two versions of this song, one in mono for the single release and one in stereo for the album.

A PLACE TO CALL MY OWN

A DELICATE fragility makes this brief snippet one of the album's most effective cuts, with Banks and Gabriel relatively free from encumbrance, until the dreaded strings ooze back to envelope it all in candy floss. Gabriel's lyrics have a sombre, sepulchre tone as he sings of a child in the womb.

Edsel CD Disc 2

PATRICIA

'PATRICIA' was the first recording that the group made together. An attractive acoustic guitar leads the way on this 1967 demo with its 'recorded in a bedroom' sound. As Tony Banks has said: "Some of these tapes are copies of copies of what were not very good recordings in the first place." A pleasant and melodic instrumental, it lilts along in 3/4 time. This first surfaced along with other demos and A- and B-sides on the *Genesis Archive 1967-75* boxed set. 'Patricia' was the tape that the pre-Genesis group of Charterhouse boys gave to Jonathan King and which encouraged him to give them a chance in the record business.

TRY A LITTLE SADNESS

MORE FUNKY piano from Tony eases Peter into a solemn and secretive ballad performance which briefly slips into Tamla Motown groove. Amidst the soulful overtones are some typically amusing Gabriel-esque lyrical touches. When the girl, who is causing Peter so much angst, takes her Dalmatian dog for a walk in the street, he hopes that she won't cry "When it comes to bite your feet".

SHE IS BEAUTIFUL

A STRONG and funky piano figure launches Peter into a wonderfully biting piece of youthful humour and cynicism as he teases the girl, describing her as "Cool as ice... a nervous wreck... you're breaking up now, breaking up your life into little pieces". He warns how "vanity arrives with fame" in a a sophisticated piece of social observation. An album of attractive Gabriel-Banks performances along these lines might have been more acceptable than the Biblical epic to come.

IMAGE BLOWN OUT

A JAUNTY Sixties pop song filled with whimsical images. Although the vocals are indistinct and buried in a decidedly rough mix you can tell that Peter is describing how a fellow can change his life, even the merry dustman going on his rounds. Piano, flute and drums invigorate the piece while you can hear the 'Wild Boars' vocal harmony group, as those responsible for the backing were dubbed.

THE SILENT SUN

THE A-SIDE version of the album track, originally released as a single in 1969. Sings Peter: "The silent sun that never shines, she is the warmth of my lonely heart... I wish you could see my love." A plaintive, appealing number, with an attractive melody it could yet be a hit if revived by an appropriate artiste. As the surging strings fade away, Banks' piano re-states the theme in a poignant coda.

THAT'S ME

ORIGINALLY the B-side to 'The Silent Sun,' this was included on later versions of the album. Gabriel's lyrics reveal obsessions with inner conflict, sadness and confusion that would become a hallmark of his work. He sings plaintively: "I look into the sun and see a reflection of a sad and lonely shrivelled man – that's me, and that's how I know it's always going to be." The words are delivered with an intimate whispering quality. The theme of a demented, deformed old man would return in Genesis imagery again and again, even long after Gabriel had departed.

A WINTER'S TALE

THIS WAS the band's second single release, released in May 1969. Gabriel excels here with a warm, cosy vocal delivery. The arrangement places heavy demands on the band but the concept is good and you can hear Peter yelling 'Now!' a familiar battle cry in the Gabriel lexicon.

ONE EYED HOUND

CHANTING background vocals and the rare use of lead electric guitar gives this a tad more funk than most of the album's material. The use of echo on Gabriel's cry of 'One eyed HOUND!' is somewhat overdone, but it was all part of the learning curve.

This was issued as the B side of 'A Winter's Tale' and if nothing else encouraged the band to think hard and try again.

WHERE THE SOUR TURNS TO SWEET

THE ORIGINAL 1968 demo version of a song that was the first track on the original vinly album and became the second track on later re-issues.

IN THE BEGINNING

ANOTHER 1968 demo that reveals how the band developed and worked on their ideas. A persistent piano motif encourages Peter to sing with greater exhuberance as he puts together some striking couples. "It has begun – you are in the hands of destiny!" he proclaims like some gleeful prophet of doom. Acoustic guitar, bass and and a tambourine join in the fun of greeting a 'newborn world' and a newborn band.

IN THE WILDERNESS

THIS IS Genesis as nature intended. Gabriel's vocals in all their youthful purity are given strong but sensitive accompaniment by Banks' forthright piano chords and the drums are suitably dynamic as the piece develops amidst crashing waves of intensity. "All I hear is music" chants Peter once more without the impediment of strings, yet to be added to this rough mix. He is given vocal harmony support by David Thomas an early friend and supporter. A fascinating glimpse into the sound of a band full of promise and still hiding out in the music biz wilderness

ONE DAY

ONE OF the finest song collaborations twixt Banks and Gabriel of the Sixties or any other decade. The 1968 rough mix has both grace and urgency, its mood redolent of 18th century drawing room life. Yet it starts in quite a hip and knowing way as Gabriel sings "Don't get me wrong, I think I'm in love..." a truly captivating opening shot. However, as the classical piano sets the tone, you can imagine a love lorn Peter gazing out of the French widows over acres of field and woodland , promising "One day I'll capture you and call you to my side", a notion that most maidens would find hard to resist. Only the Wild Boars backing group brings a note of discord to this pretty scene.

IMAGE BLOWN OUT

THE BONUS Disc of the Edsel Deluxe Edition concludes with another 1968 mix, this time of a song that bounces with charm and optimism. As Peter's vocals tend to be drowned by the piano and drums one wonders why a 'better mix' wasn't done in the first place. You can only imagine that 'rough mixes' are done by rough men, Desperate Dans, unshaven, clumsy and keen to finish their work in a hurry before the studio and the nearest pie shop closes.

Trespass

Original UK issue: Charisma CAS 1020, released October 1970.
CD Charisma CASCD 1020, released June 1988. US ABC Records ABCX
816, October 1970. Re-issued Definitive Edition Remaster, Virgin
CASCDX 1020 summer 1994.

GENESIS RETURNED TO THE FRAY IN 1970 WITH A NEW MANAGER, Tony Stratton-Smith, who signed them to his independent Charisma label after seeing them play a gig in March. The group had spent the previous five months rehearsing in Dorking, working out a stage act and preparing songs for a second album. By now the band had left school and decided to become a professional outfit. They also had a new drummer. John Silver was replaced by John Mayhew, recruited through an advertisement in *Melody Maker*.

The band had played quite a few gigs during September 1969, at youth clubs and colleges and were slowly building up a following, quite fanatical in its devotion. After completing the new album in July, guitarist Anthony Phillips and drummer John Mayhew both quit. perhaps unable to see the glittering future that lay ahead. In August 1970 Phil Collins, a former child actor who had played drums with a group called Flaming Youth was recruited through another ad in the *MM*.

Later, in December 1970, the departed 'Ant' Phillips was replaced by guitarist Steve Hackett and the classic Genesis line-up was in place. However *Trespass* had been completed too soon to benefit from these changes.

The new album was produced by John Anthony, who had worked with another Charisma act Van Der Graaf Generator, and recorded at Trident Studios, London, during June and July. More confident and dynamic than the first album it included an astonishing seven minute opus 'The Knife.'

Recalls Tony Banks: "*Trespass* was completely different from *Revelation*. By this time we had played live quite a bit and every song on the album had been performed on stage. We had a selection of at least twice as many songs as appeared on the album, and the versions changed rapidly. We had another song called 'Going Out To Get You', which was the same length. We cut out a whole section to make the album version of 'The Knife'. This started a whole new era of music. We were trying to do something different, that nobody else was doing at the time, which was extended pieces. It set us off on a new road. We had decided to go professional between the first two albums. The original drummer didn't want to do that, so we found John Mayhew. I can't say we were very pleased with the final results. We were always hypercritical."

The band wasn't satisfied with the production, although they got on well with John Anthony.

Says Banks: "We didn't know what we were doing and put too much on each track. We were let loose with 16 tracks, having done the previous one on a four track machine. We'd have six guitars running at the same time, and the vocals were very quiet. Nevertheless there were a lot of good things on that album and it started us on the direction we carried on with ever after."

Trespass had a distinctive and attractive cover with art work by Paul Whitehead that depicted two figures peering through a castle window. A jewelled, serrated knife stabbing through the design, added to the air of mystery and intrigue. It was a vastly superior package and even though it failed to get into the charts, *Trespass* sold a respectable 6,000 copies worldwide. The band were greatly encouraged and says Banks: "We got quite a response live and we were building up a following all around the country."

LOOKING FOR SOMEONE

GENESIS make a great leap forward with *Trespass*. Gone are the hesitant, nervous imperfections that flawed their first album. From the instant Peter Gabriel intones, in a surprisingly rough edged voice, the opening remarks: "Looking for someone... trying to find a memory in a dark room", we hear an artist and a band charged with a mission. The Genesis roaring on this astoundingly sophisticated opening shot is clearly determined to carve its own unique musical path.

The results of hard gigging and long hours of rehearsal are immediately apparent as the band, powered by new drummer John Mayhew, launch into a piece that is virtually an orchestral arrangement, a thousand times more dynamic and exciting than the limp strings and brass that encumbered previous efforts. The team effortlessly copes with complex unison passages, leaping into tempo changes taken at a gallop, and contrasting these with delicate, desultory guitar chords and caressing organ notes. There is a dramatic climax, and Genesis is born at this instant.

WHITE MOUNTAIN

A SHIVERING intensity is created by the opening guitar notes as Peter embarks on a picturesque story that unfolds rather like a children's radio play with musical accompaniment, as he sings of foxes and wolves and kings. He also introduces the flute to proceedings, most effective during their calmer moments. The detailed and descriptive lyrics would provide fans hours of listening pleasure as they pored over his innermost meanings and intentions. This was a crucial part of Genesis' grip on the imagination. As ever, Gabriel tosses in a few quirky asides, in this case some insouciant whistling as Banks completes his rhapsodic Hammond organ statements.

VISIONS OF ANGELS

B Y NOW Genesis had completely ditched their attempts at writing three minute pop songs, and had gone for broke as creators of full scale musical poems. The closest they get to a hook line is Peter's cry of "Visions Of Angels" during this piece of contrasting delicacy and savagery. Some have compared the ideas here to the imagery of poet William Blake. The Hammond organ is virtually an orchestra in Tony Bank's hands and he creates a constantly changing ebb and flow of moods and themes. The vocals drop out a bit in the mix and Peter sounds somewhat strained at times, but this adds a feeling of angst and desperation, often at the heart of his best performances. The wonder is that the band was able to remember all of this to repeat the performance at nightly gigs, presumably without any of the properly written charts conventional musicians would demand.

STAGNATION

I T WAS ONE of the tactics of Genesis' quickly developing stage act at this time to play gentle acoustic guitar numbers with tinkling piano in the background, to lull onlookers into believing they were hearing a folk group. Then the band would gradually add lead guitar and drums until they reached a roaring, aggressive climax that would at first entrance and then stun their audience. This was the sort of piece they played at The Friars Club, Aylesbury, 'home' for the band, from their first appearance there on April 13, 1970. "I want a drink to wash out the filth," sings Peter mysteriously before this minor epic sweeps towards a grand finale with Mayhew's drums rolling sonorously.

DUSK

ASTONISHINGLY subtle and devised with a shining brilliance, shorter, less celebrated pieces like 'Dusk' were overshadowed by the more famous Genesis epics. Nevertheless this has all the elements that helped make the band so unusual and appealing. Built mostly over chiming guitar chords, interspersed with crystalline notes from a triangle, this flows like water through a twisting channel. Sings Peter with a voice so delicate he sounds like he's handling bone china while walking on eggshells: "If we draw some water, does the well run dry?" There are snatches of unison flute and Spanish guitar, and no single idea is allowed to dominate. Anthony Phillips and Mike Rutherford blend their acoustic instruments with apparent ease. However the strain of seeking perfection on these intense recording sessions would lead to Phillips to quit the band soon after.

THE KNIFE

"NOW!" YELLS Peter again, using his favourite word to introduce a song he later explained was: "An aggressive number about a revolutionary figure on a power trip." This was the most powerful and exciting arrangement Genesis had developed thus far and it became hugely popular at live shows, when in its full glory, it could last for up to 19 minutes. Perhaps not surprisingly it failed to chart when it was released as a two part single in January 1971. It would have been hard to envisage this cut down for *Top Of The Pops*. Yet, it has a throbbing urgency that is hard to resist. Hammond organ sets off at a gallop, bringing terror in its wake. "Stand up and fight, for you know we are right!" chants Gabriel as he rides a charging war horse into battle. In a lull before the fighting there is a breathtakingly quiet passage, with beautiful flute notes cascading over a simple bass line.

Each member of the band is called upon to contribute his individual skills in a selfless way to sustain the music. This is quite unlike the situation in most rock bands where the individuals tend to fight each other to establish dominance. It couldn't be said that Gabriel was over-exposed either, as the vocal parts are quite severely rationed. While Mayhew came in for some criticism later, his drumming here is dynamic and enthusiastic, propelling a difficult and exacting arrangement towards a wild and frantic ending. This was the jagged, cutting edge of Genesis, all the more deadly for coming from such civilised company.

Nursery Cryme

Original UK issue: Charisma CAS 1052, released November 1971.
CD CASCD 1052, released September 1985. US Charisma CAS 1052
(distributed by Buddah).
Re-issued as Definitive Edition Remaster Virgin CASCDX 1052, 1994

A CRUCIAL ALBUM WHICH SAW THE BAND TAKE ANOTHER GIANT STEP with the arrival of Phil Collins to strengthen the rhythm section, and Steve Hackett to flesh out the guitar sounds.

Tony Banks and the rest of the band had been racked with anxiety in the wake of Anthony Phillips' sudden, unexpected departure, but the new drummer cheered them up from the moment he arrived with his buoyant, wisecracking good humour. He was just the right personality to prevent the band sinking into self-imposed gloom when things went wrong. A brilliant drummer, he could hold his own in the vocal department too. Steve Hackett was quite introspective and laid back, but this too suited the band, who wouldn't have welcomed an over-the-top heavy metal showman. Hackett's playing combined both melodic charm and outbursts of unexpected violence.

Recalls Tony Banks: "By this time we had lost Anthony Phillips which was a sad blow for us. But we decided we would carry on and get a new drummer at the same time. We auditioned 15, all of whom were reasonably good but Phil was definitely the best. We played as a four-piece for a while as we couldn't find a guitarist. That's why I started playing more than one instrument at a time. I had to play all the guitar parts of the *Trespass* songs on a fuzz-toned electric piano! Just before we did *Nursery Cryme*, we found Steve Hackett. Even with two new members, the album is surprisingly similar to the previous one."

Production was by John Anthony, assisted by engineer David Hentschel, who would produce later Genesis albums.

The album boasted a superb cover designed by Peter Whitehead. Inspired by opening track, 'The Musical Box', he painted a yellow-hued, strangely disturbing scene. A Victorian maiden, resembling Alice In Wonderland armed with a croquet mallet, stands bestride a massive lawn that stretches to infinity and is littered with severed heads. Work went ahead on the album while the band were off the road, due to Peter Gabriel breaking his ankle during a leap into the audience while performing 'The Knife'.

THE MUSICAL BOX

IN A masterstroke Gabriel enters this song as if it has already started, and we the listeners are arriving late during his performance. The whole piece is full of repressed sexuality and violence, and Gabriel toys with the lyrics with fastidious fascination. The most simple lines about 'Old King Cole', are rendered chilling, and phrases like "and the nurse will tell you lies", leap out from a nursery room drama that builds up in tidal waves of manic energy.

Although Tony Banks would later state that this album was similar to *Trespass*, the presence of the two newcomers is immediately obvious. Phil Collins brings a whole new dimension with his dynamic percussive playing, pushing the band with relentless drive and rock solid sense of time. Even during the quiet passages, you can hear his sticks rattling off closed hi-hat patterns that are far slicker than anything his predecessors could manage. Peter brings astonishing sensuality to his pronouncement of the key word "flesh" before embarking on an orgy of shouting from the rooftops, "Why don't you touch me, now, now, NOW!" The band returns, with Steve Hackett's guitar well to the foreground, providing the first real competition for the keyboards. Together they create a power in the ranks unimaginable only a few months before. The guitar whips up

manic sounds and Phil flies as they reach a crescendo and staccato coda that must have left them all amazed and breathless. It might still make you want to stand up and cheer this track, 35 years after its creation.

FOR ABSENT FRIENDS

IN THE midst of some pretty strong and violent musical overtures, this is a pleasing interlude in which Phil Collins makes a distinguished vocal début, The rest of the band drop out, leaving the 12-string guitarists (Rutherford and Hackett), to strum and pick behind Phil's touching vocals. The song is a brief, unfussy observation about a pair of widows attending church and thinking melancholy thoughts of loved ones lost. A nice touch, that allows a reflective moment before the onslaught to come.

THE RETURN OF THE GIANT HOGWEED

A FINE piece of what is called "programme music' in classical circles, encapsulating both Genesis' dark humour and love of story telling. The idea was based on the true case of the invasion of England by giant stinging weeds that grabbed newspaper headlines in the early Seventies. It was a perfect subject which encouraged Gabriel to devise some suitably comic lyrics. As the band lash out amidst a dense foliage of rhythm, Gabriel hacks away in his best declaiming style, telling how a Victorian explorer brought the pesky weeds back to the Royal Botanical Gardens at Kew, where their seeds spread, "threatening the human race". Gabriel has some pretty tricky lines to negotiate, including "They all need the sun to photosensitise their venom", and "still they're immune to all our herbicidal battering".

However he takes delight in skipping around this lugubrious tale, while the band cut loose with some jazzy unison flute and guitar, dancing over flawless drumming. Phil flips casually from swing to a marching beat, and there is a pause for some balletic piano before the final menacing crescendo from the entire cast. Collins' cymbals slash scythe-like at the organic growths all around him, but there is no hope. The Giant Hogweed lives.

SEVEN STONES

A N OLD man makes his reappearance in Genesis lore, this time revealing to the world his profound belief that the secret of success and good fortune is based purely on random events and chance. A Mellotron looms eerily over proceedings, adding to the gloom. Tony Banks was one of the pioneer users of this now obsolete instrument, which employed pre-recorded tapes to emulate the sound of an orchestra. A strangely mournful and inconclusive piece.

HAROLD THE BARREL

G REAT fun with a cast of comic characters that gives the whole band a chance to join in. This is the Genesis equivalent of a Carry On film, except that it is both funny and surreal. A news reader tells how a "well known Bognor restaurant owner" disappears – after cutting off all his toes and serving them for tea.

The Mayor, a Man from the Council, Mr. Plod, and the British Public all demand retribution, while his mother, 67-year-old Mrs. Barrel pleads for him not to jump off a window ledge because: "Your shirt's all dirty and there's a man here from the BBC". But Harold, in a moment of high drama, is determined to end it all and shouts defiantly: "You must be joking. Take a running jump". It's the sort of good humoured escapism that perhaps the band could have developed, to further amuse the populace.

HARLEQUIN

T WINKLING acoustic guitars return to support vocal harmonies that are closer in spirit to Crosby, Stills & Nash than British progressive rock of the early Seventies. A good example of the way Genesis music could bend and flow without recourse to ceaseless battering. No drums, no blasting lead guitar, just a steady, almost dainty rhythm to support a picturesque, poetic theme.

THE FOUNTAIN OF SALMACIS

O^{N AN} album that sparkles with great dramatic achievements, 'Musical Box', 'The Return Of The Giant Hogweed' and 'Harold The Barrel', it was fitting that the band should attempt to cap it all with a major, extended piece. This has particularly good production, with special emphasis placed on surging power chords from a band that played like an orchestra. However the vocals are a bit lost at times, and this tale of Hermaphroditus and his encounter with the wood nymph Salmacis and his/her subsequent curse upon the waters, is perhaps too elaborate to be instantly compelling. Yet it is a piece that repays frequent listening and Steve Hackett contributes some dominant guitar themes that cut through the convoluted arrangement. Collins' drums sound strangely 'tubby' at times, possibly as a result of using beaters instead of sticks, but as the whole piece surges towards a majestic conclusion, this miniature overture shows astonishing sophistication. It remains an impressive example of collective achievement few rock bands could equal then, or now.

Foxtrot

Original UK issue: Charisma Records CAS 1058, released October 1972;
US Charisma CAS 1058 (distributed by Buddah), re-issued on Charisma
CASCD 1058 July 1986.
Definitive Edition Remaster, Virgin CASCDX 1058, summer 1994

THE GREAT TRIO OF CLASSIC EARLY ALBUMS WAS COMPLETED BY *Foxtrot*. It delighted fans and finally attracted the full attention of the music press, which had been somewhat slow in catching on to the Genesis phenomenon. Packed with innovative ideas, it included two of their most celebrated works, 'Supper's Ready' and 'Watcher Of The Skies'. These coincided with the development of Peter Gabriel's increasingly theatrical stage presence, in which he used masks and costumes to act out various roles.

Foxtrot was produced by David Hitchcock and recorded at Island Studios, London during August 1972. Recalls Tony Banks: "This was a major leap forward. It was such a sweat to make this album. The first producer we had was called Bob Potter who Charisma had brought in. He was with us for a few days and really didn't like what we did at all! He particularly didn't like the opening to 'Watcher Of The Skies'. He said: 'We don't need this, it's awful.' It was uphill stuff, so we got rid of him. He was fine about it. He said: 'I don't like it, so I'm not going to do it.' We didn't like what he was doing either, so we were happy to get rid of him. We got in David Hitchcock. He wasn't really right either and didn't know what was going on. We had to work around him all the time. He was a nice enough guy, but in terms of sound we disagreed very strongly. Despite all that, the album produced some of the best things of all. We had just done the first bit of 'Supper's Ready' with the original engineer and then we did the last half with John Burns as engineer. Suddenly there was power and excitement and I came out of the studio for the first time wanting to listen to something over and over again.

"'Supper's Ready' was vastly better than anything we had done before. I was really pleased it got a lot of attention live. In the studio we found two bits of guitar were out of tune, so we had to slow one bit down and that still irks me when I hear it now. It sounds awful! But 'Watcher Of The Skies' became a classic live song even before we recorded it. There was a Mellotron introduction where we opened the whole show, which became our trademark. We had white gauze curtains behind us and dry ice, when it wasn't such a cliché. With the UV light and Pete's make up, it was a very strong opening. I thought all the songs on that album were good. It was kinda similar to the previous two albums, but a lot better and I really thought we had got something down on record that sounded like what we were trying to do. I still think is sounds good and 'Supper's Ready' was one of the best works from the early days. There were no weak songs on this album and the group was really working together as a unit."

WATCHER OF THE SKIES

A TRULY astounding performance by the band at a peak of inspired creativity. There were few more dramatic moments during a Genesis concert than when Peter Gabriel donned his famed batwings and glared at the audience with luminous eyes as he became... the Watcher of The Skies. Here is the best version they could manage in the studio at this time, and despite the limitations of early Seventies' technology, it still retains its power and excitement. The Mellotron sets the scene with minor chords filled with menace. The volume drops as Rutherford's bass builds up a staccato, insistent rhythm gradually joined by restless drums, ready for Gabriel's grand vocal entrance. He tells his tale of the Mysterious One, contemplating the fate of a departed human race, while all around him guitars howl mournfully and the band create a war chant of despair. There are overtones of Gustav Holst's 'Mars' from *The Planets Suite* in the band's use of strident, single note rhythm, but the theme and the execution is all Genesis. A particularly inspired moment comes when drums and guitar answer Banks' *sotto voce* chords in a chilling exchange before the almost unbearable momentum is resumed, finally resolved by a great roar from Collins' rolling tom toms.

TIME TABLE

L IGHT relief after the pounding excitement of the previous track, on this gentle but stirring pop song. Gabriel sings at his most expressive, without having to cope with over complex imagery or too many difficult words. Built over a kind of pedal rhythm from the acoustic piano, there is an intriguing middle section where Mike Rutherford's bass picks out melodic notes in the upper register behind delicately plinking piano.

The lyrics have poetic depth and tenderly evoke a bye-gone age of kings and queens, ultimately banished by war and conflict.

GET 'EM OUT BY FRIDAY

ONE OF the most popular numbers in the stage set, this is a kind of radio play set to music. Genesis introduce more Dickensian characters to their roster of heroes and villains. This time 'Winkler', a bailiff in the employ of property developers Styx Enterprises, is the man Genesis audiences liked to boo, in his attempts to evict Mrs. Barrow and family, on the orders of the hated John Pebble. This was written at a time when Peter Gabriel was undergoing real life landlord problems, and is full of biting satire. Even when the family agree to leave their home for a flat in Harlow New Town, they discover their rent is raised again. Worse is to come. When they reach the year 2012, genetic engineers order that all humans must be restricted to four feet in height, so more people can be packed into the tower blocks. Anyone over that height has to go! Amidst all the comic lines (including the bizarre voice of Genetic Control, that sounds like Phil Collins), there is some superb ensemble playing from the band, full of jazz-rock fusion rhythms, interspersed with cascading flutes and more suitably mournful Mellotron.

CAN-UTILITY AND THE COASTLINERS

THE SEA makes an early appearance as a Genesis motif, a theme they would explore many years later in 'Home By The Sea'. But this is a strange tale indeed, ostensibly about King Canute, but one wonders if it is actually about Peter Gabriel, as he tells of a singer wary of flatterers and tired of singing. It is indeed a mysterious tale concluding with the abrupt lines "See a little man with his face turning red. though his story's often told you can tell he's dead." While the listener can puzzle over the inner means of the lyrics, the band offers a more direct example of their astonishing musical growth. Although new recruit Steve Hackett seems held in check, when he makes his contribution it is always vital and telling. Here he manages a brief solo before locking into a tricky unison passage with the vocals.

SUPPER'S READY

FOLLOWING straight on from 'Horizons' a short but nonetheless attractive Steve Hackett solo acoustic pieces, with some nifty harmonics, comes Genesis' most celebrated epic, which took up the whole of side two of the original vinyl album. The pieces is sub-divided as follows: (1) Lovers' Leap, (2) The

Guaranteed Eternal Sanctuary Man, (3) Ikhnaton And Itsacon and Their Band Of Merry Men (4) How Dare I Be So Beautiful? (5) Willow Farm (6) Apocalypse In 9/8 (Co-Starring The Delicious Talents Of Gabble Ratchet) and (7) As Sure As Eggs Is Eggs (Aching Men's Feet).

A 12-string guitar plays a beautiful melody to create a romantic mood before Gabriel sings 'Lovers Leap' with its soulful cry of "Hey baby, don't you know our love is true." The song is curiously at odds with the rest of the lyrics which becomes increasingly manic. Acoustic guitars beaver away, then an electric piano joins in the fun as the *danse macabre* begins. Peter breathes a lover's greeting: "It's been a long time. Hasn't it" with gentle understatement, as the band finally make their appearance on 'Sanctuary Man.'

Each piece tends to segue seamlessly into each other, as the musical moods change, but there is pause for thought and reflection. Children's voice chant a nursery rhyme during 'Sanctuary Man', then Peter heralds a clash of dark forces. "Killing for peace... bang, bang, bang!" he yells as the combined forces of Hackett, Rutherford, Banks and Collins march into action. A sudden halt creates a cliff hanging moment of tension before the main refrain is repeated.

Gabriel's gift of extracting maximum meaning and sensual effect from well chosen words is exemplified on 'How Dare I Be So Beautiful?' when in the aftermath of battle he says: "We climb up the mountain of human *flesh*." The final line of this piece "...Narcissus is turned to a flower," concludes with "A Flower?" The phrase was given much greater emphasis during live performances. It was the signal for gasps and chuckles from the audience as Gabriel appeared dancing in tight black trousers with a huge flower wreathing his head, launching him into the camp and comic 'Willow Farm'.

Gabriel, growing ever more surreal. chants over a suitably silly march, "There's Winston Churchill dressed in drag, he used to be a British flag, plastic bag.. . what a drag." This piece of eccentric nonsense, much in the tradition of Edward Lear and John Lennon, stops in its tracks with a cry of "All change!"

'Apocalypse' begins with doomy chords, heralding an Elizabethan style serenade on flute and guitar. This is supplanted by a grinding, angular organ solo over a pounding, relentless rhythm in 9/8. Phil's drums skitter around the Hammond as Tony's stabbing notes become increasingly hysterical during a lengthy instrumental interlude.

Bells chime and the snare drum rolls as Gabriel sounds a return to the theme from 'Lover's Leap.' The dénouement of this massive work is reached with 'As Sure As Eggs Is Eggs', where the tempo reverts to a slow but steady rock beat, with huge notes from Mike Rutherfor's bass pedals underpinning an exultant guitar hymn. It sounds like the whole band is waving farewell, but the piece ends abruptly, right up against the stop grooves of the vinyl album. It's not a good ending, considering the epic scope of the piece, which suggests they simply ran out of tape. 'Supper's Ready' explores the complexities of human relationships, the threat of external forces and the ultimate power of love to heal.

Selling England
By The Pound

Original UK issue: Charisma CAS 1074, released September 1973;
re-issued on Charisma CASCD 1074 February 1986. US Charisma FC
6060 (distributed by Atlantic Records).
Definitive Edition Remaster Virgin CASCDX 1074, Summer 1994

WHILE THE BAND'S PERSONNEL REMAINED INTACT, THERE WERE CHANGES afoot on this album that marked a transition towards a new era. Naturally expectations were high, and Genesis fans at home were in a fever pitch of anticipation. However, the band had yet to make much of an impact in America, and they may have been thinking ahead to ways of rationalising their approach. Certainly they could not be expected to continue producing elaborate Gothic works like 'Supper's Ready', nor even 'Watcher Of The Skies', ad infinitum. Instead they began to devise shorter, more self-contained radio friendly songs, while retaining their musical standards.

Certainly *Selling England By The Pound* was the best produced album so far, with a markedly improved sound quality that elevated Gabriel's vocals out of the mush of overdubs. Perhaps the simplicity of Genesis Live (see Live Albums section) had shown what could be achieved. The new work was produced by John Burns and Genesis and was recorded at Island Studios during August 1973.

Among the innovations was a change in artwork with a cover painting by Betty Swanwick, while Mike Rutherford introduced an electric sitar to his armoury of instruments. Phil Collins' vocal work was increasingly evident and he sang solo the moving ballad 'More Fool Me', co-written with Mike Rutherford, which became a big hit at live shows. The album also yielded their first hit single 'I Know What I Like (In Your Wardrobe)' which won them world-wide recognition and remained a favourite in the Genesis show for years.

An edited version entered the UK chart at number 21 in April 1974. The album distinguished itself by getting to number three in the UK, and gained the band's first entry into the US album chart, at number 70. All this activity boosted their back catalogue and *Nursery Cryme* entered the charts after 18 months.

Remembers Tony Banks: "We wrote the whole thing in one go over six weeks, then went in and recorded it, and it was quite a difficult session. It was hard to get things going. 'I Know What I Like' was good and the second half of 'Cinema Show' worked well. 'I Know What I Like' had a nice feel and a strong chorus. There was one track I didn't want on the album and have never liked, which was 'After The Ordeal', an instrumental piece by Steve. I remember having a lot of arguments about that. I didn't want it on. Peter didn't want it on. But unfortunately Peter weakened his case because he didn't want the end of 'Cinema Show' on either. So we couldn't agree amongst ourselves and put the whole lot on and had a ridiculously long side."

When the band played the new album to their manager Tony Stratton-Smith, it was the first time that he didn't seem that excited by what they had given him. He was worried about the increased use of instrumentals. In fact the album was a success, as Banks recalls: "Of course it produced a hit single and 'I Know What I Like' eventually got to number three in the charts. It changed our status and we were able to headline tours. We had found our feet. This was a long process. We're talking 1973, four years after we had started and a lot of groups had come and gone by then! This did well for us in England but we weren't doing anything in the States. And nothing much changed for us with the next album."

DANCING WITH THE MOONLIT KNIGHT

PETER Gabriel's voice leaps out from the shadows on a piece that seems to mourn the passing of some mythical England as the country enters into the commercialised, strife torn world of the uncertain Seventies. Little did Gabriel and Genesis know what lay in store in the Eighties and Nineties, not to mention the New Millenium. However, the line "*Selling England By The Pound*", seemed to touch a political nerve, even if the lyrics now seems dated, with fleeting references to Wimpy hamburgers and Green Shield trading stamps. The band plays at tremendous speed, urged on by Collins' dazzling drums. Steve Hackett introduces some amazing guitar effects. It's all much tighter, brighter and better organised, and 'Knight' concludes with an ethereal section that ebbs and flows in a sound wash of pristine beauty.

I KNOW WHAT I LIKE (IN YOUR WARDROBE)

STRANGE whining noises like a helicopter taking off herald Gabriel's quaintly matter of fact spoken introduction: "It's one o'clock and time for lunch..." This is the band's first straight ahead pop rock song, with a stomping, steady beat and hook lines galore. A kind of African tuned drum produces a distinctive note behind the chanted chorus, where Gabriel and Collins combine. Even though this is a great pop song and a deserved hit which helped transform the band's fortunes, there is nothing ordinary about its conception.

The lyrics are rich in imagery and full of comic surprises. What were average pop fans to make of the line: "Me – I'm just a lawn mower. You can tell me by the way I walk." They loved it and Genesis fans were mostly delighted to see them gain public recognition.

FIRTH OF FIFTH

MOST successful of the major works on the album, this starts with crashing left hand piano notes and a delicate right hand melody before the band joins forces in a rather obvious 'edit'. Peter offers some ringing phrases like "The scene of death is lying just below", and plays a flute duet with the key-boards. In the background it's possible to detect a howl from Phil that sounds like an early ancestor of 'Mama'. The swirling patterns developed by Banks and Hackett here would become familiar to fans at the band's increasingly grandiose stadium shows.

MORE FOOL ME

AFTER ALL the bluster of 'Firth Of Fifth' this is a stunning contrast and a telling lesson in the power of simplicity. Phil Collins takes the vocal here with this poignant tale of a damaged relationship, sung to a simple acoustic guitar. It was written by Collins and Mike Rutherford while sitting on the steps of Island studios and later became Phil's featured vocal spot on the subsequent tour. In many ways it is the most effective item on the album and forshadows Collins's future solo career.

THE BATTLE OF EPPING FOREST

AN OVERBLOWN attempt to introduce a note of realism and modernity. A real life gang fight over territorial rights, widely reported in the newspapers, encouraged Genesis to produce a wordy but strangely dull monologue that is not helped by the flat production. In fact the whole album

The classic Genesis line-up in 1974 *(from left to right)* Phil Collins (drums, vocals), Tony Banks (keyboards, backing vocals), Peter Gabriel (vocals, flute, percussion and topless posing), Steve Hackett (guitars), Mike Rutherford (vocals, guitars, bass). *(Peter Mazel/Sunshine/Retna)*

Nursery Cryme introduced Phil Collins and Steve Hackett to Genesis in 1971. Peter Whitehead designed the iconic *Alice In Wonderland*-style cover.

Peter Whitehead's surreal painting for *Foxtrot* (1972) inspired Gabriel to wear a red dress and fox head on stage, causing a sensation among fans.

It wasn't meant to be a 'live' album. Despite protestations from the band *Genesis Live* was a hit in 1973, capturing vintage versions of 'Watcher Of The Skies' and 'The Musical Box'. Peter in devilish red box headgear lurches over the bass drum the band liked to hide.

'A flower?' Peter's petals were part of the performance when he sang the camp and comical 'Willow Farm' during 'Supper's Ready'. *(Armando Gallo/Retna)*

A new style of cover art, with a symbiotic painting by Betty Swanwick, intimates a calmer, more mature musical approach than the Gothic madness of yore on *Selling England By The Pound* (1973).

Peter Gabriel's Rael character was a tormented soul, as the triptych of scenes from *The Lamb Lies Down On Broadway* 1974 album sleeve reveals.

Tony, Phil, Peter, Steve and Mike gear up for *The Lamb Lies Down On Broadway* epic album and tour in 1975. *(LFI)*

Here comes...The Slipperman. This ugly critter went on tour with Genesis in 1975, warts and all. He is believed to be the artist known as Gabriel. Just one of many bizarre costumes Peter wore during 102 performances of *The Lamb*...
(James Fortune/WireImage)

Peter, Tony, Phil, Steve and Mike ward off a cold snap while promoting 'The Lamb Laid Down On Broadway' series of show, February 1975.
(Jorgen Angel/Redferns)

After Peter Gabriel had packed his 'Slipperman' costume and left, Phil Collins took over as premiere vocalist and master of ceremonies. *A Trick Of The Tail* (1976) with Phil at the helm proved a huge success.

Central Park, New York City, February 1976, with Bill Bruford, ex-Yes drummer (far left) joining Genesis for their first U.S. tour sans Peter Gabriel.
(Michael Putland/Retna)

A bearded Phil Collins sporting a Showco sweater, 4 January 1977.
(Getty Images)

Former Weather Report drummer Chester Thompson (right) replaced Bill Bruford as Phil's percussion partner in time for the 'Wind And Wuthering' tour in January 1977. *(Harry Goodwin)*

Phil Collins had gravitated to the position of Genesis' frontman by 1978. *(Alain Dister/Redferns)*

Mike Rutherford, 'the quiet one' of Genesis, was responsible for many of their songs as well as providing a veritable sound garden, often utilising this unique Shergold double neck guitar with its 12-string option. *(Alain Dister/Redferns)*

Genesis onstage in 1978. The previous year's *Seconds Out* had been a faithful document of the band's stage show. *(Alain Dister/Redferns)*

'And Then There Were Three'. Tony, Mike and Phil, pictured in 1980 two years after the departure of guitarist Steve Hackett.
(HKN/Rex Features)

lacks dynamics and the sense of surging urgency that characterised their work hitherto. But 'The Battle' made a good stage piece and there was one good joke: "There's no one left alive – must be a draw." The piece is littered with characters, none of them as memorable as Harold The Barrel.

AN EPILOGUE to the battle. with rhapsodic piano introduction and a pleasing duet between Banks and Hackett. The latter incidentally is shamefully underused throughout the album. The curious unwillingness of any of the band to push their particular skills or put their individual stamp on proceedings is probably the reason for the sense of a collective stand-off that prevails.

THE CINEMA SHOW

ROMEO and Juliet go to the pictures, while the band accompany their exploits with pieces that hark back to 'Musical Box'. There are no musical surprises here and little drama, but the piece does take off during a driving jazz-rock instrumental passage where at last Collins' drums catch fire and the band hits a groove. 'Cinema Show' like 'Firth Of Fifth' would sound much better live in concert.

AISLE OF PLENTY

BARELY concealed references to Tesco, Safeway, Fine Fair and other supermarket chains are heard on this throwaway piece, which fades out as Phil and Peter recite bargain offer prices. It's not surprising their manager felt a tad disappointed when he first heard an album that has touches of brilliance, a hit song and a Phil's stunning vocal debut, but lacked cohesion and Genesis' indefinable magic.

The Lamb Lies Down On Broadway

Original UK issue: Double LP Charisma CGS 101,
released November 1974; re-issued on Charisma CGSCD 1 86407 1986.
US Atco SD 2-401.
Definitive Edition Remaster, Virgin CGSCDX 1 summer 1994. Re-mixed
5.1 Virgin April 2005

GENESIS' **MOST AMBITIOUS WORK THAT ULTIMATELY LED TO THE SHOCK** departure of their much loved singer, and proved a watershed in their career. At the time of release great hopes were pinned on its success. After the years of development and struggle, this was to be the blockbuster that elevated the band to mega star status. However, it was based on such a complicated, demanding story line, developed independently by Peter Gabriel, that in the short term it proved hard for audiences to understand and accept and caused friction within the group. Gabriel's comic fantasy stories that had so endeared him to fans lost their appeal when taken too seriously and spread over four sides of an album.

But all was not lost. The work yielded at least three good songs, and it became the basis of an impressive stage show that delighted fans. Peter produced some of his most bizarre costumes for *The Lamb* show, including the lumpen and misshapen 'Slipperman', and weird looking 'Lamia'. The production utilised three projection screens which helped illustrate the story, while Peter acted the role of the main character called Rael. At one point there were two Raels on stage, and as Peter intended, audiences found it hard to distinguish which was the real character and which one was actually a dummy.

The album was recorded at Glosspant, Wales with the Island Mobile studio and was mixed at Island Studios, London during late summer 1974. *The Lamb* was produced by John Burns with Genesis and engineered by David Hutchins, while the sleeve was provided by Hipgnosis, the design team famed for their work with Pink Floyd.

Across some 23 tracks Gabriel told the story of Rael, the spray gun toting Puerto Rican punk from New York City. It was a radical departure for Peter to attempt a theme set far away from his beloved England. It was full of references to contemporary American figures like Caryl Chessman and Marshal Mcluhan.

Dealing with problems of alienation and split personality, Gabriel found it difficult to explain the complexities of the story which revolved around the hero undergoing some sort of out-of-body experience as he walks along Broadway. Even when he wrote an explanatory note for the LP (reproduced in the subsequent CD booklets), they were so long and printed in such small type, they proved difficult to read. As the project grew the band seemed uneasy and restless at Peter's dominance, both on stage, in the studio and in the press. He had taken responsibility for *The Lamb* and its subsequent failure in terms of sales and reviews was unsettling and frustrating.

The creation of the work had been fraught with difficulties. Peter had just been offered the chance to write a film script for Hollywood movie maker William Friedkin (director of *The French Connection* and *The Exorcist*). There were two crucial weeks when he missed out rehearsals for the new album, while he was waiting to see if the film project would get off the ground. In the end Gabriel returned to Genesis.

When it was decided they would do a double concept LP, Peter insisted on writing all the lyrics himself. His wife Jill was expecting their first child at the same time, and the pressure on Peter to devise enough lyrics was intolerable.

Eventually the album was completed and was a Top Ten hit in the UK album chart. They played the *Lamb* show at some 102 performances across America and then in France and at Earls Court in England in 1975. The shows themselves drew huge crowds and were largely deemed successful, even if most found the story impossible to comprehend. But Peter had already secretly decided to leave the group. When it was finally made public at the end of the tour, his fans were greatly shocked and many doubted if Genesis could survive without him, which only served to enfuriate the rest of the band. To those who knew only half the story it seemed as if Peter was being forced out, but there were many causes and the gamble with *The Lamb* had not helped his case.

Recalls Tony Banks: "Being a double album this was much more difficult for people to promote and it was the only album to sell less than its predecessor. It didn't do so well in England as *Selling England*, and it didn't sell in America. We tried with singles off the album, but couldn't get any off the ground. We suffered from lack of radio play. I thought 'Carpet Crawlers' had a good chance. Making this album started off great but it turned into hell by the end. And by the time we had finished we were fed up with it, because it took so long to do – about five months. But the result was one of the strongest we had ever done. I think it has so many strong moments although it's flawed and has lots of things wrong with it.

"I'm not so crazy about the story myself. It was just something to hang songs on, although the individual lyrics are great. The album spawned a very important live show, and we went to town with all the effects. It's funny, people look back on that album now and say it was a classic from the early days, but it got unanimously bad reviews at the time. Nobody liked it and it went down badly. Pete wrote the story and all the lyrics. This was a bone of contention. We had internal problems within the group, so it wasn't the happiest time for us."

In the aftermath Gabriel launched a highly successful solo career and with Phil Collins taking over as lead singer, Genesis would prosper for another 20 years.

THE LAMB LIES DOWN ON BROADWAY

TONY Banks' rhapsodic piano introduction heralds this daunting and controversial work. The main theme provides some of the most memorable moments from the whole enterprise, and it was to survive in the band's set for years to come. In their eagerness, the band played *The Lamb* in its entirety on an American tour, before the album had been released, and as Phil Collins recalled, this left audiences intrigued but bemused. By the time the band reached Los Angeles more fans had heard about the Lamb epic and consequently gave it a rousing reception. The title piece owes its origins to The Drifters' 'On Broadway' and develops a stomping urban beat. Hackett and Collins drive proceedings forward, adding to the sense of urgency as Peter sets the scene with emphatic vocals.

FLY ON A WINDSHIELD

PETER intones the thoughts of the hero character Rael, as he experiences forebodings of death and alienation on New York's Times Square, surrounded by the careless surging masses. "I'm hovering like a fly waiting for the windshield on the freeway", sings Gabriel, his voice given a bold new clarity and presence. When the band played the album live in New York there was allegedly some hostile reaction from real Puerto Rican punks who couldn't understand what these English guys were trying to say about them. Acoustic guitar and shimmering vocal harmonies presage a sudden burst of rhythmic violence as the piece segues into a mysterious instrumental section. The drums kick with John Bonham style power as the guitar riffs angrily. Peter embarks on a semi-spoken rap before Rutherfordian 12-string guitar brings calm and peace.

BROADWAY MELODY OF 1974

A GENTLE 33 second acoustic guitar passage over sustained chords links 'Fly' and 'Cuckoo Cocoon' and doubtless served as a useful pause at live shows, to enable the band to limber up for the next demanding arrangement. It was also useful when Peter gave audiences at the start of each show a brief outline of his imaginative story, by saying: "It tells of how a large black cloud descends into Times Square, travels out across 42nd Street, turns into wool and sucks in Manhattan Island. Our hero, named Rael crawls out of the subways of New York and is sucked into the wool, to regain conscious-ness underground."

CUCKOO COCOON

G ABRIEL'S sensuous flute sere-nades Rael as he becomes cocooned in the 'powdered wool', and the strange experience on Broadway begins. It's a richly melodic chiming composition in the 'Musical Box' tradition.

"Wrapped up in some powered wool, I guess I'm losing touch. Don't tell me this is dying, cos I ain't changed that much. I wonder where the hell I am – in some kind of jam," laments Rael, finding himself alone in an unreal world where there is no sign of life. "But I feel good," he declares as the flute returns and the guitars and key-boards extemporise a lilting refrain.

IN THE CAGE

A HEART beat emanates from the drums as the narrator intones "I've got sunshine in my stomach like I just rocked my baby to sleep... but I can't keep me from creeping sleep..." The madness piles up for Rael as dressed in a white costume he is caged in a cave full of stalag-mites and stalactites. Tony Banks whips up an angular, almost hyster-ical Hammond organ riff backed with humming bass lines as Peter/Rael yells "Get me out of the cage!" Eventually Rael's 'cage' dissolves and he is left to spin help-lessly in space. But not before the band moves into a furious jam with Phil's drums picking up the tempo behind Tony Banks' sustained keyboard notes, Steve's buzzing guitar and Mike's manic bass. Live performances of this number proved even more exciting than the studio version.

THE GRAND PARADE OF LIFELESS PACKAGING

"IT'S THE last great invention left to Mankind," proclaims Peter in an electronically processed voice, as the piano commences a march depicting automatons going about their work. He describes the 'grand parade of lifeless packaging' a product being made by Rael's brother John in some dreary factory. Amusingly deep baritone voices accompany Peter's anguished depiction of a bizarre production line as the band seem to chance upon Fritz Lang's *Metropolis*.

BACK IN N.Y.C.

ANGRY vocals are matched by an angular motif set up by layers of keyboards and guitars over a tricky drum pattern. This must have caused much screaming at rehearsals to get right. The ensemble theme has an hypnotic effect that builds to a ferocious climax. Gabriel's vocals are seemingly sung underwater, perhaps amidst the subways and drains of New York City. The strongest feature here is the stabbing staccato interplay between singer and band backed by Phil Collins's explosive drumming.

HAIRLESS HEART

A REFRESHINGLY gentle instrumental interlude brings relief after the angst of 'Back In N.Y.C.'. There is a kind of surgical precision about this piece whose title evokes strangely disturbing imagery.

COUNTING OUT TIME

ONE OF the album's strongest songs is sung with Peter's characteristically saucy humour as he sings about his favourite 'erogenous zones'. Hackett offers raunchy lead guitar riffs and there are some wonderfully strange noises and effects, presumably courtesy of Eno who lent his skills to the production. Great fun and this was a song that deserved to be a hit single.

THE CARPET CRAWLERS

A NOTHER excellent ditty, on which Phil Collins' provides superb backing vocals, as well as a rolling thunder of drums. His marching rhythm keeps perfect time. Meanwhile, a deep toned Gabriel sounds as if he is suffering from a head cold as tells more about the mysterious lambs wool and a golden fleece that promises peace. Sometimes referred to as 'Carpet Crawl' the piece contains the insidious hook line sung in close harmony: "We've got to get in, to get out". A firm stage favourite, it builds to a satisfying climax and is full of subtle musical and lyrical references.

THE CHAMBER OF 32 DOORS

EMOTIVE lead guitar and ferocious tom tom and cymbal crashes open the doors of perception then Rael, who is now in despairing mode, sings simply: "The rich man stands in front of me, the poor man behind my back. They believe they can control the game... I need someone to believe in, someone to trust." Town and countrymen are compared and the country men came out on top in the general estimation. Warm Hammond organ notes provide a sympathetic accompaniment as Rael searches for the right direction and Collins points toward hope and sanctuary with his encouraging drum beats. "Help me find the door! Take me away!"

LILYWHITE LILITH

A NEW character, Lilywhite Lilith is recruited to rescue Rael from his cave and take him through the tunnel of night. "Don't be afraid" she says cheerfully as the band embark on a short but extraordinary blend of themes, tones and rhythms.

THE WAITING ROOM

WIND chimes are introduced and various noises off supplied by Eno produce some intriguing effects. It sounds like hungry cats demanding fresh supplies of food. This is accompanied by breaking glass, moans and gurgles topped by the sort of foghorn that would have guided the Queen Mary into dock. Great fun, although not the sort of noises you'd want to hear while waiting in a room for the family doctor.

ANYWAY

TONY Banks' delightful grand piano is one of the pleasures of a piece which advances the story by creating an attractive melody. "Oh boy I feel no pain. I guess I must be driving myself insane," muses Rael. The full band blast out powerful unison chords while Banks keeps the recurring piano motif firmly in place. As sophisticated orchestral writing and performing 'Anyway' takes some beating.

HERE COMES THE SUPERNATURAL ANAESTHETIST

THE ANAESTHETIST is death personified but Hackett's

vibrant guitar work here is very much alive. Steve delivers bold and incisive licks, accompanied by tricky drum fills involving complex interplay on the hi-hat and snare drum, a feat best appreciated by other drummers. The guitar explodes with a fury here that shows how Steve could have galvanised the whole *Lamb* concept if the lead guitar had been given a little more space.

THE LAMIA

THE LAMIA are crucial figures to the tale, with their heads and breasts of beautiful women who live in an ornate pink water pool. After inviting him to swallow some of the waters, they seem intent on feasting on Rael's flesh and blood. As Gabriel resolutely delivers the details of an increasingly impenetrable tale Hackett gets a grip with some firm guitar statements over the all embracing Hammond organ. Rippling piano offers a moment of serenity and the snake-like Lamia are heard going about their curious business, nibbling at flesh. "The lights are dimmed and once again the stage is set for you," sings Peter significantly, as the guitar and drums signal another crescendo in which every note has its place.

SILENT SORROW IN EMPTY BOATS

DELICATE mood music, interspersed with heavenly choirs give listeners time to pause and reflect as they aborb a piece of work that anticipates the birth of ambient music a decade later. It fades away as the empty boats float down the river and slip from our view.

THE COLONY OF SLIPPERMAN (ARRIVAL /A VISIT TO THE DOKTOR/ RAVEN)

JAPANESE influences are heard as strange stringed instruments twang and chirrup and temple blocks clip-clop. Rael chances upon the Slippermen, described as 'Slubberdegullions on squeaky feet' and the band leap to their feet to welcome the latest strange visitors to an increasingly overcrowded Broadway. The concept of the Slipperman gave Peter a chance to wear a suitably repulsive costume on stage. As Peter describes the hideous spectacle there is a touch of his old humour as he adopts a suitably slobbery voice. During 'The Raven' curious phrases pop up like "It's a yellow plastic Scooby-doo". Tony's synthesiser wails to good effect and the band get into an up-beat frenzy, Phil bashing his echoing snare drum with renewed fury. Unusual time signatures, beats that stray across the bar and constantly shifting moods make one wonder how Genesis could possibly remember so much complexity without having some sort of brain implant.

RAVINE

ERIE effects, and howling winds suggest 'Ravine' might make ideal film music and this subtle vignette certainly helps paint a picture of abandonment and loss.

THE LIGHT DIES DOWN ON BROADWAY

HEADING for home now, Rael seems torn between destinies, freedom from the rat race, or imprisonment in the strange surroundings he chanced upon while strolling along Broadway. There is a reprise of the original theme as the narrator questions the juxtaposition of dreams and reality, as this prodigous work draws towards a close. The flute signals a chirpy optimism over the marching drums.

RIDING THE SCREE

BURBLING synthesiser offers thrills and spills while perky drumming enliven a segment in which Rael is surrounded by tumbling rocks as he tries to overcome his fear and aims to survive his strange ordeal. "You got nothing on me" comes a lone American cowboy voice in the final moments.

IN THE RAPIDS

DELICATE guitar ushers in a slow, thoughtful tender song which tells how Rael's brother John, is seen drifting down a river out of sight. "Striking out to reach you I can't get to the other side" is the agonised cry as the brothers shoot the rapids of life.

IT

THE BAND leaps into some of their most spirited playing of the entire double album. Peter Gabriel seems to offer a coded explanation for sticking by his project by whispering during the final moments: "It's only knock and knowall, but I like it". And so ended the first era of Genesis. Fans and even its sternest critics eventually came to like and understand better the aims and intentions behind *The Lamb*, a concept that was many years ahead of its time. A new generation would get a chance to appreciate its significance when the entire album was remixed in 5.1 sound for release in 2005.

A Trick Of The Tale

Original UK issue: Charisma CDS 4001, released February 1976;
re-issued on Charisma CDSCD 4001 1986. US: ATCO SD 36-129;
Definitive Edition Remaster, Virgin CDSCDX 4001 autumn 1994

A **CRUCIAL ALBUM FOR GENESIS, THEIR FIRST SINCE THE DRAMATIC** departure of Peter Gabriel. If anything the shake up encouraged the band to focus their material and re-double their efforts. Produced by David Hentschel, it had a more dynamic sound quality that had been lacking on *Selling England By The Pound*. It marked the start of the modern era of Genesis, showing how recording technology was advancing during the mid-Seventies.

Tony Banks' tasteful use of synthesiser compensated for the loss of Gabriel's flute, while the vocals and drums had much more presence and power.

Hentschel was a good friend of Phil's and been the band engineer when they recorded *Nursery Cryme*. A musicians himself, he assisted Tony Banks in developing the use of synthesiser and was responsible for the new, improved drum sound.

The material was credited to the individual composers, so there was no confusion. In the past many fans had assumed everything had been written by Peter Gabriel. On this new album the lyrics to songs like 'Entangled', and the block busting 'Squonk', were clearly the work of Mike Rutherford and Tony Banks, while the latter wrote the poetic title track. This was the album that showed the band was capable of standing alone, ready to successfully face a world that thought they had no future without Gabriel.

Says Tony Banks: "Both the previous albums weren't that easy to make and this one was such a relief and breath of fresh air for us. Peter Gabriel had decided to leave and we had great fun, writing and recording it. There was a lightening of the load, and we needed to streamline the band. Obviously we were very sad to see Pete go because he was a very close friend, but something had to give somewhere. It has been proven it was good for Peter and good for the band for him to leave at that point. It gave us all a bit more room.

"The press didn't know he was going to leave, but we all did. The atmosphere wasn't as good in the band as it had been in the early days. We didn't want him to leave but we had to make the best of it it. It presented an interesting challenge. The publicity for the band had been very wrapped up in Peter which slightly tended to overemphasise his contribution. He was obviously important, but he wasn't The Band as some people saw it. We had every confidence we could produce a good album, but we found it difficult to get people to take us seriously, until they had heard it."

Work began before Gabriel's departure was made public, and before they had found a new singer. They actually tried out one new recruit, but he found the keys difficult. Phil Collins volunteered to sing on 'Squonk', which was one of the first pieces written for the new album. He sang it with tremendous verve and the band and their producer knew they need look no further. The only problem was how to cope with live performances when Phil was tied to his drum kit. The answer was to bring in Bill Bruford (ex-Yes), who joined the band for their first North America tour without Peter. Their first show was given in London, Ontario, Canada when Phil had to sing in front of 4,000 dedicated Genesis fans. He was an instant success, proving he could communicate with audiences as well as Peter.

A Trick Of The Tale also sold more than any of their previous albums. It went to number three in the UK and reached 31 in the US *Billboard* chart.

Says Banks: "It was our biggest record and the first one to make any kind of sense in America. We actually got our one and only good review in the *NME*! The music was certainly more immediate and had striking riffs like 'Dance On A Volcano'. 'Squonk' had a very heavy drum sound and it became a stage favourite. It was the simplest song we had done. This was the start of a much happier period for us. *The Lamb* had killed us to play it on stage and some of the songs didn't work well live but this album produced a whole lot of instant stage hits."

DANCE ON A VOLCANO

DAYLIGHT is shed over Genesis with the assistance of David Hentschel. The band make a huge leap forward, instantly apparent from the famous opening notes of 'Dance On A Volcano', best described as: "Blip, blap, blip, blap, diddle a dah!" The band comes alive and Phil's voice, powerful, and confident gets to grips with lyrics that are detailed without being convoluted. While the old Genesis had begun to sound lost and in danger of repeating itself, the 'new' trimmed down band is brisk and to the point with fresh ideas. "Let the dance begin," says Phil, in devilish tones.

ENTANGLED

A PRETTY ballad by Steve Hackett and Tony Banks with 12-string guitars providing melodic jangle while Collins assumes command and adds his own backing vocals. Perfectly formed and delicately performed, it has all the fragile tension of a Simon & Garfunkel song. 'Entangled' drifts into a hauntingly melodic climax with resounding chords, before the soporific guitars gently fade away.

SQUONK

THIS WAS the first piece on which the new band jammed, while they were waiting for the official announcement to the world that Gabriel had gone. Phil was yet to assume his vocal duties in Peter's place, but once recording began, it was obvious he could effectively take over.

The drumming is transformed, the jazz-rock style replaced by solid back beats and heavy, carefully placed tom tom fills. A big, fat rocker, it is the sound of the future, not just for Genesis but for pop music in general.

MAD MAN MOON

PHIL'S vocals are accorded a clarity here rarely achieved on any of their previous albums. A pleasant pop song, composed by Tony Banks, and performed with unaffected simple sincerity. A delightful piano interlude creates a pastoral mood before Collins returns to sing over a difficult time signature. With its shifts in mood and tempo, it sounds suitable for a stage musical production. It is a sobering thought that music of this depth and quality simply could not be conceived let alone recorded for a commercial album today.

ROBBERY, ASSAULT AND BATTERY

COLLINS used to act out this tale of a murderous safe cracker on stage, wearing a flat hat and carrying a bag of swag. It's a much better constructed piece than 'Battle Of Epping Forest', with simple, direct lyrics, delivered with a hard edged reggae beat. This became the basis for the first ever Genesis promo video with Phil playing the role of the burglar and the rest of the band as policemen.

RIPPLES

CRYSTAL clear vocals are the fore on a piece that recalls some of the calmer moments of 'Supper's Ready'. Well placed bass notes from Mike Rutherford at his most sober and reflective underpin the melody while the acoustic guitar carefully picks out an Elizabethan style folk melody. "Sail away" sings Phil as he tells of the face that launched a thousand ships. "The face in the water looks up and shakes her head," he intones. Steve Hackett launches into a linear melody on lead guitar matched by rippling piano.

A TRICK OF THE TAIL

THE TITLE track is a jaunty Tony Banks' composition with a strident, four-to-the-bar piano theme and a marching drum beat. It tells the story of youth attempting to escape from the gilded cage of a safe existence. Phil sings with sparkling clarity and masterful narrative skill as he tells how "Bored of the life in the city of gold he'd left and let nobody know..." It seems he is led away and put in a cage neatly labelled with the sign 'Beast that can talk.' Yet despite its curious theme and carefully written lyrics, it's still a bright and cheerful pop song with the nifty hook line "They've got no horns and they'd got no tail, they don't even know of our existence." Together with 'Squonk' this was the sort of inspired, well crafted production that would eventually unleash a flood of Genesis chart hits.

LOS ENDOS

A HIGHLIGHT of Genesis shows, this powerful, fast moving instrumental provides a triumphant conclusion to a highly satisfactory album. It commences with a few bars of desultory guitar before roaring off at breakneck speed. Themes interweave and tempos change, while the drums roar. Genesis often give the impression of jamming, while sticking to a strictly controlled and disciplined arrangement. The main keyboard part has a calming effect, while the guitars and drums do their best to achieve a kind of blissful nirvana with spurts of furious energy. Collins excels, playing with all the command of a big band drummer. While the entire band plays brilliantly on *Trick Of The Tail*, it is very much a tour de force for Phil, unleashing all his pent up skills, talent and energy.

Wind And Wuthering

Original UK issue: Charisma CDS 4005, released January 1977;
re-issued on Charisma CDSCD 4005 April 1986. US: Atco SD 36-144.
Definitive Edition Remaster Virgin CDSCDX 4005, Autumn 1994

WIND AND WUTHERING WAS THE FIRST GENESIS ALBUM RECORDED abroad, at Relight Studios, Hilvarenbeek, Holland, during September 1976. It was remixed at Trident Studios, London during October and produced by David Hentschel and Genesis. This was a period of consolidation for the band and apparent stability. Steve Hackett remained a part of the line up, although he had shown some frustration, only partly assuaged by the release of his first solo album, *The Voyage Of The Acolyte*, the previous year. It seemed he was becoming increasingly unhappy that the band wasn't making enough use of his writing.

On tour the band now included American drummer Chester Thompson (who had replaced Bill Bruford), but the personnel on studio albums would only feature the original members. Phil had seen Chester play with jazz fusion band Weather Report at a London concert, and was keen to take him on the *Wind And Wuthering* tour. He played his first concert with Genesis on January 1, 1977 at London's Rainbow Theatre, and stayed with the band for the next 15 years.

The previous post-Gabriel album had won the band a lot of new listeners, who found their music more acceptable and less off-the-wall. It was hoped the upward spiral would continue. Yet the new album sold about the same in Europe, and only marginally improved in America. Tony Banks felt that *Wind And Wuthering* harked back to the days of *Foxtrot*, in that it re-introduced melodramatic themes, on such compositions as 'Eleventh Earl Of Mar', 'One for The Vine' and 'Blood On The Rooftops'. While it contained some of their best work, it had been a difficult album for the band, due in part to the tension created by their guitarist.

"This was a much more ambitious album," recalls Tony Banks. "It is one of my favourites from the Seventies, because it had the most adventurous music and it was pretty easy to make. We were quite prolific at this stage and we had three songs left over. The album ended up a bit heavier than was originally intended because we left off three of the lighter songs, which ended up on an EP called *Spot The Pigeon*.

ELEVENTH EARL OF MAR

A SONG about the Scottish Jacobite, John Erskine Mar, the 11th Earl, who started out as a Whig, and because of his constant change of sides, earned the nickname 'Bobbing John'. He headed the Jacobite rebellion of 1715, was defeated at Shereffmuir and died in exile in France. Presumably Banks and Rutherford had been studying his history rather intently. This rousing epic makes a good vehicle for Collins to recount a strident tale of battle. A splendid introduction, with grandiose keyboard chords and swooping guitar licks, sets the Earl on his proposed journey from Perth to London in search of promised victories, while his son cries reproachfully "Daddy, you promised."

ONE FOR THE VINE

GUITAR and piano set up the mood with a hauntingly simple theme statement. Ostensibly it's another story of a wild eyed fanatical leader, ordering his men into battle and certain death. It suggests that Genesis were out to recapture the story telling spirit of yore and it's a highly successful strategy. According to Tony Banks, the song is an allegory about someone realising he has finally become the person he once aspired to be, only to discover there is nothing special about him at all.

Steve Hackett pops up briefly and a lively instrumental passage mimics the clanking sound of swords in action. "In his name they could slaughter, for his name they could die," roars Phil. "Though many there were believed in him, still more were sured he lied, but they'll fight the battle on." A cleverly wrought composition 'One For The Vine' survived in the stage act for many years to come.

YOUR OWN SPECIAL WAY

AN OUTSTANDING pop song from Mike Rutherford that has all the best virtues. Richly melodic, with an emotive hook line, Phil sings it with great passion and real enjoyment, over a gently swaying rhythm. It commences with Mike's acoustic guitar, Phil picking up the mood by gently intoning "Go far enough and you will reach a place where the sea runs underneath... I've sailed the world for seven years and left all I love behind in tears." And then he confesses, "I've been alone long enough... you have your own special way." Beautifully conceived and tastefully executed, this is one of the high spots on the album. 'Your Own Special Way' is a marvellous performance that retains its understated emotional impact nearly 30 years on.

WOT GORILLA?

CHIMES, triangles and bells, rattle, shimmer and chime in the build up to an intriguing instrumental interlude that provides a pleasingly surreal contrast to the more elaborate set pieces. A solid drum rhythm and furious Hammond organ reach a crescendo over a striking theme , before shimmering bells and chimes return for a trance inducing fade-out finale.

ALL IN A MOUSE'S NIGHT

A CAT AND mouse tale, told with relish by Phil. There's a loving couple in bed you see, and a mouse invades their privacy, only to meet his fate at the hands of the household cat. Says the male bed partner enjoying his moment of intimacy: "Got to get beside you 'cos it's really cold out here. Come up close to me, you'll soon be warm, hold me tightly like we're sheltering from a storm." Meanwhile the mouse muses: "Into the night and out of this hole, maybe find me a meal." His arrival in the bedroom causes ructions but his escape plans are thwarted by a cat that "comes in for the kill... hard luck mouse." This amusing tale is concluded by the cat boasting that he delivered a *coup de grace* to a monster mouse was "ten feet tall". There is a Disney-ish cartoon quality about this whimsical bedtime story, complemented by a bouncy theme and powerful drumming.

BLOOD ON THE ROOFTOPS

AN ACOUSTIC guitar ushers in Phil's thoughtful ruminations on the paradoxes and banalities of comfortable suburban English life, while watching the latest news on TV. A play, a film or the Queen's Christmas speech are clearly preferable to a diet of dimly understood wars and the politics of distant lands. It's an unusual, sombre vignette that utilises the newly developed string synthesise to create an orchestral wash of sound.

UNQUIET SLUMBERS FOR THE SLEEPERS... ...IN THAT QUIET EARTH

A TWO pronged instrumental, which commences with an mellow, autumnal feeling before a snare drum roll launches the band into a high speed jazzy work out. Staccatto bass drum work accents the theme which slows to half tempo before accelerating into an exciting climax full of unexpected 'rests' and blasting big band style explosions. It's an exuberant, action filled arrangement and while the album seems dominated by sober, serious themes, here is a chance for the players to get their rocks off.

AFTERGLOW

'IN THAT Quiet Earth' flows into 'Afterglow' which has nothing to do with The Small Faces' tune of the same name. Collins sings poignantly "For now I've lost everything – I give you my soul" over a crisp but solemn beat. A nostalgic warmth permeates a relaxed but stirring song that presages the sort of highly personal ballads that would illuminate Phil's subsequent solo career. "I miss you more" he sings and you can feel the depth of his personal feelings. In a strange way this album encapsulates the different interests of the individual band members. There is Phil Collins' yearning to sing and write his own songs, the need for Mike Rutherford to write well crafted pop tunes, Tony Banks' vision of Genesis as a palette for orchestral expression and Steve Hackett, a virtuoso guitarist in search of his freedom. All would be resolved and revealed.

And Then
There Were Three...

Original UK issue: Charisma CDS 4010, released April 1978;
reissued Charisma CD 800 059 2 May 1983; Charisma CDSCD 4010
August 1991; US Atlantic SD 19173
Definitive Edition Remaster, Virgin CDSCDX 4010, Autumn 1994

THE DEPARTURE OF PETER GABRIEL HAD BEEN A GREAT SHOCK TO THE system but Genesis soon learned to live without him. Phil Collins proved such a all-powerful replacement the band went from strength to strength. Their albums sold better and tours of America and Europe grew to blockbuster proportions. They continued to write imaginative material, even if some of the magic had gone. They were a better equipped, more mature band, but there were still undercurrents of dissent. Steve Hackett had contributed a great deal to their sound with his unique guitar style, but felt frustrated that more of his compositions weren't being used. Genesis never was a guitar-led band in the traditional sense. Nevertheless they benefited from his work. It was a shame that Steve couldn't communicate his feelings of frustration to the others. In the end he just decided to leave. It left many wondering how the band would cope as a three piece.

The title of the new album hinted at a closing of the ranks. Once again Genesis was up against world opinion, and they were determined to show their mettle. Banks, Rutherford and Collins were the core of the band and as soon as they had finished mixing 'Seconds Out' they went into the studio to make their most successful album to date, which went Gold in the US.

In keeping with the times, the band decided against lengthy performances, and cut eleven relatively short tunes. It was an understandable reaction against their old image, all part of their constant process of change. One of the tracks, 'Follow You Follow Me' was their first UK Top Ten hit, which helped introduce the band to a much wider audience.

Work began at the Relight Studios, Holland in September 1977 with producer David Hentschel. Says Tony Banks: "Coming down from four to three members after Steve left was uplifting and easy to cope with. We had a little more to make up in terms of the guitar playing and sound. Mike had to spread himself more as a guitarist. Looking back, most of this album was written by Mike and I individually and we felt we were playing a bit as session guys on each other's songs. 'Follow You Follow Me' was one of the few group-written tracks on that album and it was pretty successful. There were some nice things like Mike's 'Deep In The Motherlode', but it's not of one of my favourites. I can't work out why! The best tracks were 'Undertow', 'Follow Me' and 'Say It's Alright Joe'.

"We were right in the middle of the punk era by then and everyone was predicting our downfall, so we produced our biggest selling album to date and a big hit single. More people began to listen us than ever before. Funnily enough, punk rock helped us as many bands didn't survive and we had a lot less competition in our area. I thought we were better, so this confirmed it in a way. We had complexity, but the basis all our songs was in melody and sound."

DOWN AND OUT

AN EXPLOSIVE, driving drum beat pushes and shoves through a tough talking exposé of music business attitudes. A bossy record company executive breaks the bad news that someone is about to be dismissed. "None of us are getting any younger, there's people out here who could take your place." The message gets worse for the victim as the boss explains "So it's with regret I tell you now, that from this moment on, you're on your own!" Phil seems to relish this earthy satire with its booming bass line and strident theme.

UNDERTOW

TONY Banks' romantic bitter-sweet love song includes the poignant line "So the days they turn into years and still no tomorrow appears". It sums up the feelings of those who fear that time is slipping away and great ambitions have yet to be fulfilled. There is some comfort though, as Phil sings "We're safe in each other's embrace, all fears go as I look on your face." Surging chords and deep, rumbling bass notes give a hymnal quality to an outstanding composition that hints at a life in danger of being cut short by "a blow that fate has struck upon you." Full of subtleties and tender lyrics, here is a song that takes time to blossom, like a rare orchid.

BALLAD OF BIG

A STIRRING wide-screen epic tale of bravery starring one 'Big Jim Cooley' and set in the Wild West. It seems that Big Jim is a deputy sheriff and cattle rancher who is "feared by everyone". He allows himself to take on a bet in a saloon bar, one fateful night and is goaded into taking a herd across the plains in dangerous, hostile territory. Just when it seems their mission is accomplished the cowboys are attacked by Red Indians and Big Jim dies "with his boots on, next to his men". Phil Collins tells how his ghost roams the plains and as far as Jim is concerned the bet is still on. A lively story, it works surprisingly well.

SNOWBOUND

A PRETTY song of children at play in the midnight snow with innocent lyrics that perhaps conceal a deeper meaning. Phil sings Mike Rutherford's composition with due respect and reverence as he calls out with childlike glee "Hey, there's a snowman!" He adds with a touch of parental wisdom: "They say a snow year's a good year, filled with the love of all who lie so deep." An avalanche of keyboards engulfs the icy melody.

BURNING ROPE

T ONY Banks' cleverly wrought piece grows more appealing with frequent plays. It has detailed lyrics and its sentiments express a rather sombre view of life, insinuating that with age one realises that "accomplishments turn to dust". Strange to hear such dispiriting thoughts from a successful young man. However, it seems the burning rope is an allegory for the life line used to escape retribution. "You climbed upon a burning rope to escape the mob below, but you had to put the flaming out so that others could now follow." The aim is is to flee "the barks of those who do not wish you well".

Emotive lead guitar work from Mike compensates for the absence of Steve Hackett and there is a yearning quality about the memorable tune.

DEEP IN THE MOTHERLODE

A NOTHER Western flavoured song in which Phil sings "Go west young man" urging a 17-year-old youth to leave home, mother and family and embark on a daring quest for gold. The band sets off at a jogging canter as the wagons roll and the guitars strike up a sprightly theme, set against a background of distant banjos. 'Motherlode' concludes, somewhat sadly, that "the golden fields that beckoned you are darkened by the years... if you knew then what you know today, you'd be back where you started a happier man." So much for gold digging.

MANY TOO MANY

A SLOW, wistful refrain, although the chorus is quite strong and the song builds towards a logical conclusion. Phil sings in reflective, somewhat bitter mood. "What I find strange is the the way you built me up then knocked me down again – why can't I leave?" There is a claustrophobic air about the performance, that suggests a prisoner prowling in his cage, or a husband trapped in a marriage. Otherwise it is a finely wrought pop song that was released as a single in July 1978 but only reached number 43 in the UK chart.

SCENES FROM A NIGHT'S DREAM

A FANTASY tale that deals with a child's nightmares about goblins and giant mushrooms. The child is called, rather oddly, Nemo and one wonders what parent would suggest such a name, apart from Jules Verne, author of 20 Thousand Leagues Under The Sea. This is 20,000 leagues from the Genesis of 'Foxtrot' days.

SAY IT'S ALRIGHT JOE

S OFTLY, softly the vocalist toys with lyrics that are very much in 'One For My Baby', mode as Phil pours out his heart out to a sympathetic barman, who pours out his drinks. "Say it's alright Joe, I need some reassurance, you never know what you might find in the night" intones the fearful singer. It's a restrained performance that starts with gentle, rippling piano and is enhanced by Mike's humming bass line. Even the album cover, with its photographic portrayal of a deepening sunset, the onset of dusk and neon lights flicking on, reflects the mood created in by this melancholic cocktail. It livens up for a more powerful instrumental section, before returning to a swirling melody of bells, chimes and sustained guitar notes, cleverly depicting the fading light and receding memories.

THE LADY LIES

T ONY Banks' judicious use of Hammond organ re-introduces a taste of old Genesis on this seductive saga about a mythical character, who is really a demon and "not a maiden fair". Even so the demon is quite alluring and Phil reflects: "Who can escape what he desires?" The band starts to rock and the wailing synthesiser solos becomes surprisingly bluesy as the male/victim is lured into a trap by the female/demon. The final chorus is dominated by a jazzy piano motif and some great drumming. Out demons, out.

FOLLOW YOU FOLLOW ME

FUN PERCUSSION effects, including bouncing bongoes over a samba beat, ensure that this is one of the album high spots. Phil sings the irresistible hook line to a big hit that remains one of the band's best liked songs from the mid-Seventies. The lyric and message are simple enough. "I will follow you, you will follow me... I will stay with you... will you stay with me." Such sentiments are more readily digested than any number of tales about demons and giant toadstools. As the arrangements progresses, the instrumental parts come together in a neat and satisfying resolution. 'Follow You Follow Me' was their first US Top 40 hit. It peaked at number 23 and stayed five weeks in the chart. The single fared better in the UK and reached number seven.

...And Then There Were Three earned the band a Gold Disc, got to number three in the UK charts and number 14 in the US *Billboard* chart. The album proved Genesis could function successfully in the studio as a three piece. However, out on the road they decided to augment the line-up with guitarist Daryl Stuermer, who joined in February 1978. He boosted Genesis live, playing alongside fellow American, Chester Thompson. Now they were three, but soon they were five.

Duke

Original UK issue: Charisma CBR 101, released March 1980;
re-issued on Charisma CBRCD 101, April 1985. US Atlantic SD 16014. CD:
Definitive Edition Remaster, Virgin Autumn 1994

THE BAND FACED THE CHALLENGE OF THE NEW DECADE WITH RENEWED enthusiasm. They had been buffeted by the winds of change blowing hotly through the music scene. In the wake of Punk Rock they were being written off and derided by a music press that had once supported them. Yet they had survived by showing a willingness to experiment and more importantly, their power base in Europe and America was growing. Just when it seemed 'progressive rock' bands were on their way out, Genesis were entering an astonishing new phase that would be full of surprises and see them attain a world-wide following on a massive scale. Although they were by now a three piece and would remain so in the studios throughout the next decade of their history, they augmented the band on stage, and wrote music that would incorporate all the freedom and power offered by new instruments and new technology.

On November 12, 1979 they went to Abba's Polar Sound studios in Stockholm, Sweden, to start work on *Duke*.

"We had been through the punk era and everyone had predicted our downfall and yet ...*And Then There Were Three* was by far our biggest selling album, because 'Follow You' had been a hit single," says Tony Banks. "More people listened to us than ever before. Our producer didn't like that song, but Charisma told us to release it." Reconfirming his belief that Genesis could out-ride the punk rock storm Tony added: "We never considered NOT carrying on. Fashions come and go you know."

Genesis had a long, difficult tour in 1978 and which brought to a head Phil Collins deteriorating marriage situation and by the end of the year, he was said to be in bad shape. Mike and Tony worked on solo albums while Phil went abroad and then underwent a divorce, so there was a two year gap before *Duke* appeared. "I didn't have as much material ready as usual, nor did Mike," recalls Tony. "Phil, meanwhile, had time to write stuff. We listened to it and thought it would be nice to use on a Genesis album." *Duke* marked the beginning of Phil's role as a songwriter *par excellence* and it was partly his influence through grew new adult songs like 'Misunderstanding' that saw Genesis make the move from old style prog-rock towards a more commercial sound.

However, Banks still believes the best tracks on *Duke* were those written as a group. "The standout track is 'Duchess', which was the first time we had used a drum machine on a record. Very simple, but it had a strong melody. 'Turn It On Again' was great and proved to be a classic Genesis song. 'Behind The Lines' was the first time we got into a funkier feel. 'Please Don't Ask' was written by Phil about his marriage. The only song we didn't do was 'In The Air Tonight' which we could have done as a Genesis song! 'Misunderstanding' was treated more as a Fifties kind of lyric, which we turned into a video."

Banks says that 'Turn It On Again' was originally a throwaway section used between two other bits. "We played it all again twice in the studio, 'cos it seemed so good. When we were making the album, Phil was a bit sombre and we were used to him being our main joke provider. But it wasn't a difficult album to make, and we had a lot of fun. We were very pleased with the results. The sound wasn't as good as it should have been though, and there was a great lack of bottom end."

Despite their two year absence *Duke* was the band's first number one UK album. 'Turn It On Again' got to number eight in the UK during April 1980, proving that a vast new audience was discovering the veterans as they completed a turbulent decade together.

The album peaked at number 11 in America and earned the band their second US gold disc. 'Misunderstanding' released as a single reached number 14 in *Billboard*. It was the start of the band's greatest record success in America.

BEHIND THE LINES

Bright, tight and confident, the band reveal a joyful spirit that was so obviously missing from many of their Seventies albums. The instrumental intro seems to herald a new dawn and a new decade. After the build up, spurred by crisp, battering drums, Phil finally makes his vocal entrance and the bass guitar rumbles and skitters in groovy Tamla Motown fashion, as the keyboards shout like a brass section. "I'll stay if you want me to," sings Phil.

DUCHESS

Floating in the wake of the previous stomping work out, 'Duchess' has a delicate drum machine rhythm to set up the piece – all new and daring stuff in 1980. This swirling, ambient music still sounds sleek and chic some 25 years later. After tantalising moments alone with the machine, a marching snare drum launches Phil into a soulful vocal interpretation. A mature, satisfying performance that combines all the best elements of modern Genesis – and introduces the sound and mood of Phil's subsequent solo albums.

GUIDE VOCAL

" I AM THE one who guided you this far," says Phil, leading the way into a subdued Tony Banks composition. We can but accept his direction.

MAN OF OUR TIMES

A SINGULARLY powerful piece, distinguished by a ferocious snare drum pattern that shadows a series of repetitive keyboard phrases, over a droning bass line. Phil's cries of "He's a man of our times" are barely heard above the din, Exciting and dramatic, the band manage to combine Gothic splendour with shiny techno-rock violence.

MISUNDERSTANDING

A WELL ROUNDED, satisfying soulful pop song that is in direct contrast to the remnants of old Genesis thinking apparent elsewhere on the album. The band sound like they are enjoying it too, relaxing on a groovy beat that showed just how they yearned to break free from the mould of the past. This owes more to the Apollo, Harlem, than Friars, Aylesbury and was a Top Twenty hit in the US, peaking at number 14. Phil sings about a missed meeting and a wait in the rain with affecting simplicity.

HEATHAZE

P HIL TALKS of the things that "give life meaning" in a thoughtful, considered ballad redolent of smoky night clubs, or some Left Bank café. The drums sound muffled and unusually sloppy, doubtless the intention. One never knows with these artistic chaps. The piano offers pleasant, mellifluous support.

TURN IT ON AGAIN

A WONDERFUL song, one of the best on the album, and an instant classic that became an integral part of Genesis shows henceforth, as it was invariably turned into an entertaining medley of favourite pop and soul hits. After counting in the tempo, Phil sings the memorable line "I can show you some of the people in my life..." and you wonder who they all are. The doubled up Indian war dance backing beats are irresistible, and the whole piece is beautifully arranged. As Genesis' royal fans might observe, one doesn't wish it to stop. A Top Ten hit in the UK, surprisingly it wasn't such a big hit in America, where it reached number 58 in *Billboard*.

ALONE TONIGHT

PHIL AT his most appealing on a Mike Rutherford song of loneliness that doubtless reflected Collins personal circumstances at the time. "No one cares I'm a lonely man," he says, adding "now I'm alone again." He reflects on the breaking dawn, the state of the world and his own sense of abandonment. Of course, one might think all he had to do was nip down the pub and play a game of darts. But when one is love lorn, even darts can fail to ease an aching heart.

CUL-DE-SAC

A STRIDENT Tony Banks' composition with a strong orchestral theme that launches with a stirring drum roll in the grand manner of a symphonic overture. Phil sings the refreshingly matter-of-fact-lyrics that contrasts pleasingly with complexities of songs from the previous decade.

PLEASE DON'T ASK

" PLEASE don't ask me how I feel – I feel fine," sings Collins with a trembling bottom lip that hints at tears held in check, as he contemplates the surging emotions and baffling set of circumstances that surround a break up with a loved one. Once again Collins shows how one simple song, sung from the heart with the maturity born of bitter experience, means so much more than the surreal fantasies of youth.

DUKE'S TRAVELS/ DUKE'S END

T WO BAND compositions conclude this unique album that perhaps saw off some of their older fans, but gained them the respect of a new generation. At any rate these rich instrumental pieces had all the values intact, that had stayed at the heart of the band from their earliest times.

A tidal wave of synthesisers followed by a surging current of dancing drums, launches an instrumental that seems like a logical progression from 'Dance On a Volcano' and 'Los Endos'. There is a touch of the Highland flings as the three man band get into their stride. The strident optimism contrasts with the introspective sadness of Phil's ballad contributions and you get the feeling this was inspired by moonlight and brandy. Philip sings a snatch or two in the midst of the instrumental battering and when the band returns at full tilt, such is the sense of drama you'd expect audiences to stand up and salute. The tempo doubles, guitars rock and Phil cooks at the drum kit like a man possessed as 'Duke's End' reaches an exciting climax.

Abacab

Original UK issue: Charisma CBR 1021, released September 1981;
re-issued Charisma CD 800 044 2, May 1983. US: Atlantic SD-19313
Definitive edition Remaster, Virgin, Autumn 1994

ORIGINALLY RELEASED IN FOUR DIFFERENT VINYL ALBUM SLEEVE COVERS, *Abacab* was produced by Genesis and engineered by Hugh Padgham. Recorded at The Farmyard, Surrey, Banks, Collins and Rutherford were augmented on one track, 'No Reply At All', by the Earth, Wind & Fire horn section. The song was a hit in America where it reached number 29 in the Billboard chart. The title track 'Abacab' and 'Man On The Corner', were also hits in the UK and the US. The album itself fared well, and was the group's second U/K number one and their first US Top Ten platinum album.

"This brought a radical change," says Tony Banks. "We decided to do mainly group written stuff as that had proved the strongest on our previous album. By this time we had built ourselves a studio, which wasn't actually ready by the time we did *Abacab*, so we rehearsed in the sitting room of the place we had bought. Meanwhile, during the album, Phil's solo success began to break through which took us all by surprise. Suddenly 'In The Air Tonight' was 32 in the charts and the next week it was number four and it was "Here we go!" Phil suddenly became a big star during the making of the album, but it didn't really affect the way we made *Abacab* and it certainly didn't affect our relationship together. We all knew each other too well. It's difficult to have illusions about someone you have known for fifteen years.

"We did try to avoid Genesis clichés on this album – things like always bringing in a tambourine on the chorus, and the big instrumental passages we had used on the previous five albums. So we tried some things we'd never done before, rhythm and blues tunes like 'No Reply' with horns on and 'Who Dunnit?' which was a real one-off piece. 'Me And Sarah Jane' carried on the Genesis tradition a bit. My favourite track was 'Keep It Dark' which was quite short but had a lot of atmosphere. We called it 'Odd' for its original working title. We put two bars of drums on a loop and played against it. Having our own studio enabled us to do that sort of thing. We couldn't use all the tracks and kept three back for an EP. The album sold well and made a real impact in America."

ABACAB

A POWERFUL blasting intro leads into a rocking keyboard riff that contrasts with some grinding guitar from Mike. Phil stabs out the phrases in staccato bursts, and the drums hit a back beat – you can't lose it. Tough, concise and shouting with confidence, this is Genesis geared up for the Eighties with a vengeance. Strange noises permeate the single note beat bashed out during an extended instrumental work out that gradually fades to oblivion.

NO REPLY AT ALL

TRUMPETS blare unexpectedly on a track that boils with funky energy. Never has the Banks, Collins & Rutherford Orchestra sounded so soulful. "Dance with me," begs Phil in unusually sensuous mood, while Rutherford's superb bass swoops around the melody. Despite all the innovation, it still sounds like Genesis. Hugh Padgham does a superb job fitting it all together, retaining both heat, atmosphere and clarity. "Is anybody listening?" demands Phil, getting no reply.

ME AND SARAH JANE

THE BRAIN of the drum machine is adjusted to provide a popping kind of beat, while Mr. Collins sings in harmony with himself before returning to his steam-powered kit. Padgham was determined to ensure a loud, exciting drum sound prevailed in contrast to the padded, sticky taped, muffled thuds that often passed for studio drums in the Seventies. The mood here switches from looping reggae to spaced out, floating orchestral sounds closer to the *A Trick Of The Tail* era. A strange ditty, full of surprises.

KEEP IT DARK

AFTER THE intro the tune seems to invert and set off backwards. Collins' vocals are harsh, strident and set against the sort of melody Paul McCartney might have developed during The Beatles' *White Album* period. Even twenty five years later, this still sounds very modern, and the use of repetitive block chords from the keyboards presaged the whole dance music phenomenon. At least one assumes it did. It may have been presaged by some keyboard player from Cleveland, Ohio.

DODO

YOU'D think at least twenty musicians were playing together in some vast rock orchestra to produce the breath-taking depth of sound here. Phil almost snarls the simple, emphatic vocal lines about the agitator who "Must die", bringing us an all-new, modern, aggressive Genesis. The Dodo seems to be a distant cousin of The Squonk. Phil rolls around the tom toms with slow, violent deliberation and this is possibly the closest Genesis ever got to playing funk metal. The whole piece seems to segue into 'Lurker' in seamless fashion.

LURKER

TONY Banks obtains some remarkable effects during a solo that sounds like a tipsy trombonist colliding with a set of bagpipes.

WHO DUNNIT?

POSITIVELY weird now, as the band rocket into outer space on a tune that sounds not unlike a lesser known work by Madness. Phil reverts to his best West London cockney accent and demands to know 'Who Dunnit?' This is one of the most vicious and unusual concoctions ever devised by Genesis, concluding with a massively powerful drum explosion. Manic, repetitive, it becomes quite frightening in its hypnotic intensity. And if you've ever been intensely hypnotised, you know that can be quite frightening, in a manic, repetitive sort of way.

MAN ON THE CORNER

THE DRUM machine returns to provide a gentle, probing rhythm for Collins to sing with the same touching sincerity that caused such response when he released his first solo album. A simple handclap rhythm accompanies Phil as he talks of the lonely man waiting on the corner: "What he's waiting for I don't known, but he's there every day, waiting for someone to show," sings Phil proving that a few, simple phrases and a strong melody mean so much more than all the Lambs who ever laid down on Broadway. Of course the lonely man could be waiting for a bus on Ealing Broadway, but it's unlikely.

LIKE IT OR NOT

A RELAXED, loping tempo in 6/8 time. "There's still another chance to hold on to our love because I gave you everything I had," sings Phil with great power and passion his sentiments touching at the heart strings, before the band returns, firm and reassuring.

ANOTHER RECORD

"PUT ANOTHER record on!" pleads Phil against a howling harmonica on a song larded with late Fifties style Doo Wop yet packed with contemporary sounds. It's is all a million miles from 'Suppers Ready' and shows a band determined not to be tied down to their own past glories and ready to explore and mix whatever sounds catch their fancy. *Abacab* is an extraordinary album by any standards and even more remarkable when one considers it was produced by a band that had already been making music for a dozen years. They'd done so much that was revolutionary in the past and here they were still setting standards of creativity. And there was a whole lot more to come.

Genesis

Original UK release: Charisma GEN 1, released December 1983,
reissued on Charisma GENCD 1 December 1983

WITH *GENESIS* **THE BAND FORGED ONE OF THE MOST IMPRESSIVE ALBUMS** of the early Eighties, and in the process created their most powerful and dynamic musical statement thus far. The unique style and sound of key track 'Mama' with its heavy drum beat and Phil's memorable appearance in the accompanying video as a kind of spectral, disembodied head was both dramatic and shocking. It proved that with all of the Genesis men at the peak of their creative powers, there was room for both Phil's own hugely popular solo albums, and a Genesis revival.

There was an obvious pride and confidence in the project, reflected in the blunt title, *Genesis*. Recalls Tony Banks: "This carried on a bit from *Abacab* where we put things down on tape before we worked them to death. We rehearsed in the studio, and as soon as we got something we thought was good, we put it down on tape. 'Mama' was put down as just a drum machine and a chord sequence to get the feel. It had great atmosphere on its own and didn't need anymore. Mike Rutherford's drum machine set the pattern in motion, and it sounded really good. We added more effects and Phil just improvised vocally while we were doing all this. A few lines came like 'Can you see me Mama' and then the drums came in, which was a bit like 'In The Air Tonight' but we had done that in the past.

"The sound of the drums really came from Peter Gabriel's third album on a track called 'Intruder'. Phil was the drummer at the time, Hugh Padgham was there and the sound just sort of developed. The idea of using a big drum sound excited everyone. Before that. every light beat was heard and when played very fast it just destroyed everything else, so I always liked slow, simple drum parts. I liked the way Led Zeppelin used drums. On the *Genesis* album, I really liked side one and the first three tracks. The second side was less exciting but it had some nice moments. 'Mama' was the strongest thing we'd ever been involved in. 'Home By The Sea' was good too, although it was just us improvising for hours over a drum rhythm."

MAMA

S TRANGE overtones emerge from the drum machine pattern that sets off this remarkable concoction. It's much more subtle than it sounds. Gradually the grinding beat is joined by synthesised noises that approximate the fluttering rotors of a probing helicopter. Then... Phil Collins emerges from a harsh, cruel soundscape to offer the plaintive cry of a lost soul wandering abroad in the city. The song smokes and reeks with atmosphere, as Collins pauses to deliver his famous maniacal laugh and accompanying growls. This hint of evil and despair is assuaged by Tony Banks' spiritual chords that offer relief and succour to the tormented. Somehow, during inspired moments fooling around in the studio, the musicians manage to create the image of a battle between good versus evil, man versus the machine. One can only imagine the delight that Collins, Rutherford and Banks experienced on hearing the first play back of this minor masterpiece.

THAT'S ALL

B RIGHT, light relief from the terrors of 'Mama' is offered by this joyously simple and unaffected pop song. "I loved you more than I wanted to," Collins sings, capturing in a few lines the curious pressures and dictates of the heart. The whole piece is beautifully constructed and sports a guitar solo from Mike Rutherford that can only be described as merry. This soared to number six in the US charts in December 1983 and was their first American Top Ten hit.

HOME BY THE SEA

A JAPANESE tinged melody prevails on an extended work that needless to say, went down very well in Japan, when the band toured there in 1987. A song about images, memories, nostalgia and dreaming, it drifts into its companion piece.

SECOND HOME BY THE SEA

V IOLENT storms seem to batter the home by the sea during a furious instrumental section. Listening to the pristine clarity of the production, the fury of the drums and magical mixture of keyboard and guitar effects, one wonders what the young Charterhouse pupils would have made of it all, had they been transported in time from *Revelation* to *Genesis*.

ILLEGAL ALIEN

A SOMEWHAT controversial subject for Genesis to turn into a light hearted, semi-comic video and theatrical performance. Complete with Mexican accent, and fake moustaches Phil and the chaps emulate a hubbub of aliens attempting to enter the United States. While broadly sympathetic to their plight, ("It's no fun being an illegal alien") it borders on the tasteless when the band blithely include the line "I've got a sister who's willing to oblige... she will do anything to help me to get to the outside." Mysteriously Phil veers off into a West Indian accent accompanied by a steel drum, as the background moves momentarily from the Mexican border to the Carribean. One wonders what illegal aliens think of it all. "Politically incorrect" might be their most charitable observation.

TAKING IT ALL TOO HARD

BACK ON safer ground, this is a well sung ballad over another drum machine rhythm. Collins is at his most restrained and soulful as he addresses a loved one and advises her: "The old days are gone, and they're better let alone." Sound advice that most ignore.

JUST A JOB TO DO

TRULY funky guitar blends with hammering bass on a series of interconnecting jazzy riffs a million light years from 'The Fountain Of Salmacis'. A skipping, handclapping beat urges on this tale of a hit man in hot relentless pursuit of his victim. Menacing, and rather frightening in its implications.

SILVER RAINBOW

AS TONY Banks points out, the last few tracks of *Genesis* lacks the consistent brilliance of the first four; this is rather noisy and inconclusive. A song of love on a sofa and the fumbling advances of youth, the 'Silver Rainbow' could well be a zipper, waiting to be unzipped.

IT'S GONNA GET BETTER

NOT A classic song by any means but it contains some intriguing backward notes and a clearly defined ruminating bass line. Collins sings in a high key but the lyrics are a tad non-descript. It's not the great ending one might expect from an album that begins with such power. Yet comparatively speaking, their weaker moments might be lesser mortals' highest achievements.

Invisible Touch

Original UK issue: Charisma (Virgin) GEN LP 2, released March 1986;
issued as Charisma (Virgin) GEN CD 2 December 1986.

A VIBRANT, HIT PACKED ALBUM THAT BROUGHT GENESIS RENEWED success after 17 years of work and achievement. They returned with some of their most powerful, memorable performances of highly original themes, bursting with life and energy. The band seemed to revel in their new-found enthusiasm. As if Phil Collins' own personal success wasn't enough, he proved capable of repeating it all again, combining his energy as a singer and writer, with his old Genesis friends. 'Invisible Touch', 'Land Of Confusion' and 'Tonight, Tonight, Tonight' would dominate international charts throughout 1986/87, a period during which the band embarked on a triumphant and spectacular world tour.

The album was recorded at The Farm, Surrey during 1985/86 and produced by Genesis and their alter ego Hugh Padgham. In June 1986 the album topped the UK charts while the song 'Invisible Touch' became their first single to top the charts on both sides of the Atlantic. The band would also enjoy Top Five hits in the US with 'Throwing It All Away' (number 4), 'Land Of Confusion' (4), 'Tonight, Tonight, Tonight' (3), and 'In Too Deep' (3). 'Land Of Confusion' was assisted in its race up the chart by a witty video created by the Spitting Image TV puppet makers Fluck and Law. It won them a Grammy Award for Best Concept Music Video. 'Tonight, Tonight, Tonight' was also used in a US TV beer commercial, a less distinguished treatment of a beautiful song.

The band were delighted at their heart-warming success and were very proud of the album.

Tony Banks: "*Invisible Touch* became my favourite of all the albums we had made. It was very consistent and we were very pleased that it got such a good reaction in America. We tend not to get good reviews or music business awards but when people hear our singles they think: 'This is great, I really like the sound of this!" and they go out and buy our albums to hear the rest. That was the advantage of a hit like *Invisible Touch*. It attracted more people to hear all of our music.

"Every week hundreds of albums come out and you can't expect people to listen to all of them. But we felt very strongly about this album, and everything from the cover art to the designs was bold and striking. We were confident we had done something really good."

INVISIBLE TOUCH

PURE POP, this is a joyous celebration of love, life and the mystery of human contact. 'Invisible Touch' is a magical performance set into motion by Mike Rutherford's opening guitar statements that were the original inspiration for the piece. Collins' exultant cries of: "She seems to have an een-vis-ible touch, yeh-ah!" have since echoed around a hundred stadiums. Her invisible touch threatens to tear Phil apart but the reassuring bass line hums and haws, keeping the singer and band, safely together. Tony Banks however succumbs and flies off into keyboard heaven with a delirious solo.

TONIGHT, TONIGHT, TONIGHT

MIKE Rutherford, when pressed on the subject, once said Genesis' last ambition was to record their personal "ultimate album" as most groups, including The Beatles had done during their careers. *Invisible Touch* comes closest to achieving this distinction. Unlike many of their previous albums, there isn't one sub-standard track. Hot on the heels of their most exuberant, exultant pop song, comes their most memorable rock ballad, complete with vintage Collins vocal. A big drum machine pattern is pur-

sued by a sharp snare drum roll that heralds a nagging electronic theme. Insistent and coldly cruel, it sounds like it might be at home on the soundtrack of a Helloween movie. The lyrics are alternately obscure and direct. Phil seems to suggest his love is "like a monkey... a load on your back," but promises "Tonight... were gonna make it right." Fortunately he has some money in his pocket: "I don't remember where I got it, I gotta get it to you." As the late Dudley Moore might have said: "He's got some money in his pocket, doesn't know where he got it – funny." Phil's lyrics, improvised in the studio along with most of the music, have all the impact of strip cartoon bubble writing – tight, terse and curiously potent. "Please get me out of here!" roars Phil after the band complete a series of suitably weird instrumental effects, and then... the mad monkey from hell returns. There is no escape.

LAND OF CONFUSION

THIRD hot track in a row, as Phil offers thoughtful, well intentioned lyrics which tackle the world's problems of war and chaos, written before the horrors of Yugoslavia brought strife back to central Europe and firmly onto the doorstep of the West. However Phil's worries in 1987 have a prophetic ring to them. "Now did you read the news today, they say the danger's gone away, but I can see the fire's still alight, burning into the night." The fires of war have burned ever more fiercely since Genesis pleaded: "This is the world we live in, these are the hands we're given. Use them and let's start trying to make it a place worth fighting for." Although Hugh Padgham contends the album was made up of bits of jams, taped together, this sounds like a well conceived, complete entitity. Drums rap out a staccato military tattoo while a synth bass keeps the mills of war grinding.

IN TOO DEEP

THERE is a crystalline perfection about this warm and tender song, which Phil sings at his most intimate and restrained. Every note from the Banks/Rutherford axis tells a story and has its value, from the click of a clave to the surge of a synthesiser. A few well chosen guitar chords add substance to the electronic dreamscape.

ANYTHING SHE DOES

IN STARTLING contrast to the comforting warmth of 'In Too Deep' comes a furiously fast charge into battle, with brass sounds giving the trio the effect of a blasting big band.

The digital sound quality is quite amazing as synthesisers and

drums – real or sampled – create the aural equivalent of virtual reality. Hugh Padgham and the team unleash audio perfection. It's certainly a far cry from the scratchy 78 rpm sounds that ushered in the first age of rock'n'roll. Yet it all sounds logical and effortless. The deliberately messy ending seems to signal a desire to re-introduce the spontaneous human element.

DOMINO

PRESENTED in two parts, this was accompanied by an effective video during the *Invisible Touch* tour, showing cascading lines of dominoes. Part One begins slow and pretty until an abrupt, stabbing explosion ushers in Collins with 'In The Glow Of The Night'.

The tempo doubles for Part Two – 'The Last Domino' dominated by a menacing, relentless beat as Phil sings of the perils of the world, and how the domino effect can bring unavoidable doom to all, including us supine TV watchers. "There's nothing you can do when you're the next in line – you've got to go – domino!" he yells. Now there's a cheery thought. Listeners with headphones can detect strange stereo clicks during the final exciting work out. Those with loudspeakers can stare blankly out of the window and eat a bag of chips. Well if we've gotta go, there's not much else we can do about it.

THROWING IT ALL AWAY

A FETCHING guitar introduction from Mike sets up Phil as he sings with a warbling intensity, a singularly moving and attractive ditty. The lyrics flow with a neat and clever precision, and once again it all sounds rather prophetic, in view of later developments in the singer's personal life. "We cannot live together, we cannot live apart. That's the situation, I've known it from the start... you know, I know baby, I don't wanna go." But he did. However it cannot be claimed this song applies to any particular living soul. Vocally speaking, it is however yet another example of Phil's knack of touching the raw nerve ends of human relationships.

THE BRAZILIAN

S TRANGEST and most demanding cut on an album that is packed with brilliantly conceived and executed pop songs. This is all instrumental, a re-affirmation of the band's faith in its musical past, which insists that the casual listener, ensnared by this extraordinary collection of hits, lends his ears to something a little more cerebral. And we don't mean palsy. Full of spacey sounds, and weird experimental effects, it is dominated by what sounds like a sea monster, breathing heavily and stomping up the beach. This is a Genesis style saucer full of audio secrets. Brazilian percussion rattles a furious warning, before the sea monster puffs and wheezes his way back into the ocean depths. 'The Brazilian' also made a splendid live piece and by now Genesis concerts were hugely entertaining marathons of entirely original music, backed up by the wonders of new technology from computer controlled lights, to bits of paper stuck on the stage to remind Phil of the lyrics.

We Can't Dance

Original UK issue: Virgin GEN CD3, released 1991.

DURING 1991 GENESIS BEGAN THEIR FIRST RECORDING SESSIONS TOGETHER in five years, although it hardly seemed possible the gap was so long. In the first five years of their existence there had been so much frenzied activity. But the life span of one album like *Invisible Touch* was much greater than in the past. An album's impact could be sustained for years, through a succession of hit singles, videos and major tours. The challenge now was to see if the band could repeat the trick, and with *We Can't Dance* they achieved yet another blockbuster. The new CD was packed with 70 minutes worth of music spread over 12 mature and considered songs, each with its own well defined character. There were some surprises, and there were elements of humour and drama in the lyrics and their interpretation. Yet the predominant themes were of love in crisis, fading memories and a pervading sense of sadness and anger at the ways of the world. It was the music of older but not necessarily wiser men, still grappling with the same problems that beset and concerned them in their youth.

For the first time in some years, Hugh Padgham was absent from the control desk, and the album was produced and engineered by Nick Davis. It was recorded at The Farm, Surrey between March and September 1991, and the music was entirely the work of Tony Banks, Phil Collins, and Mike Rutherford. The CD booklet was illustrated with tasteful water colours by Felicity Roma Bowers which neatly complemented the lyrics. An inside cover photograph showed the three men of Genesis sitting in a civic hall, looking glum, surrounded by the remnants of a party, Phil wearing a decidedly sad looking paper hat. Together with the sombre, reflective lyrics of the final song 'Fading Lights', it almost seemed as if Genesis were finally, discreetly trying to say good-bye.

NO SON OF MINE

TIME TICKS by as Phil narrates a singularly sad tale of a rift between father and son. Quite why the son leaves his parents, and the true nature of his crime is not explained. Could he be gay, or turning to a life of for crime? All Collins, as the boy, tells us is: "I needed a place where I could hide, somewhere I could call mine... Soon I was living with the fear everyday of what might happen at night."

Despite his good intentions – a return and perhaps an apology – his father looks him in the eye and says... well the lyrics are all provided on the sleeve. Phil's careful build up and dénouement of the theme is done with great care and skill. A painful story of rejection, strengthened by a crisp back beat.

JESUS HE KNOWS ME

A HARD hitting entertainment that became the basis of an elaborate video. Phil plays the role of American TV evangelist, introducing just the right note of hypocrisy, irony and sardonic humour. Conceived at a time of great scandal in the lives of real life TV preachers who prey on the gullible, Phil sings: "Get on your knees and start praying." The band play with great gusto, Rutherford's guitar popping and cymbals ting-ing. A Bob Marley-ish reggae interlude breaks things up before they roar back into the attack.

DRIVING THE LAST SPIKE

A MIDST all the carefully wrought compositions on the CD, this ten minute saga is perhaps the least successful. Inspired by tales of the English navvies who built the railway network in the early 19th century, it proves rather heavy going. In an attempt to offer something like the narrative epics of early Genesis, the documentary flavour palls and the subject matter must have been difficult for younger American audiences in particular to understand. Phil does his best and there are some steaming Pete Townshend style guitar chords to drive in the last spike. On British railways of course, they used 'chairs' and bolts to fix the rails to the sleepers, not American spikes.

I CAN'T DANCE

M UCH better, and one of the album's real treats and surprises. "Hot sun beating down," sings Phil breaking out into a sweat as he summons up images of life as a convict, working on a chain gang in the Deep South. It's a radical piece Genesis fans would never have expected from the band, back in the Seventies. It works though, and it is terrific. Phil sings the blues over a funky guitar while the drum machine beats time like a guard's lash on his back. Phil devised a brilliant dance routine for their video which accompanied the single. As he explained: "At drama school there was always one kid who didn't know how to move and couldn't dance. The hands and the feet just went the wrong way!" Rutherford and Banks cheerfully joined in the video fun to help make this a huge hit.

NEVER A TIME

A STAX SOUL feel permeates this pulsing ballad on which the vocals respond to spine tingling guitar. A slow, measured tread accompanies Phil as he sings pointedly, "You live your lives locked in a dream, where nothing is real, and not what it seems." It all ends abruptly, with the finality of a broken relationship.

DREAMING WHILE YOU SLEEP

THEY used to be called 'Boo Bams' – percussion instruments that have a hollow, distinctive note. They may or may not be the source of the haunting and mysterious sounds that usher in a rather chilling, cautionary tale of a driver who is involved in a hit and run accident and kills a young woman. Phil relates the story in the restrained tones of a man keeping his guilty secret. Like 'No Son Of Mine', it is cleverly direct, yet holds enough information back to make it intriguing. Who is the villain – who is the victim? All we know for sure is the culprit's admission: "I didn't stop to see what I had done." Distant Clapton-esque guitar adds atmosphere as Phil ponders: "Could I take my secret to the grave." Huge crashing drums add a note of impending doom.

TELL ME WHY

" MOTHERS crying in the street, children dying at their feet, tell me why," demands Collins bluntly at the start of an anguished outburst at the problem of world hunger. Critics often grow resentful or suspicious at what they see as 'rich rock stars' droning on about world problems as if they were saviours or had something helpful and original to say. But Genesis are in a better position than most to make constructive use of their communication skills. Phil convinces us with his direct and simple appeals. He means what he sings. 'Tell Me Why' has a worthwhile message, delivered with panache and resolution.

LIVING FOREVER

A NOTHER cleverly wrought social topic, this time concerning the obsession with health advice that bombards modern man from TV, radio and magazines. Phil concludes that the conflicting views on diet and exercise and things that are deemed good one minute and bad the next, are just part of a ploy to dominate the minds of the masses. "You think you know better... you just want to rule over everybody's lives," he avers. What sound like wire brushes, deftly played on the snare drum set up the beat, but according to Phil: "I can't play the brushes!" Yes, it's that old sample machine back in action.

HOLD ON MY HEART

A TENDER, soft and attractive song, sung by Phil at his more caring and romantic. Love songs used to be bawled out by brash night club performers in tuxedos. Phil sings of love in a proverbial flat cap, with a glass of Brown ale, and a packet of chips, and it all seems so much more meaningful. There is the residue of a soul guitar groove ticking away in the background, and warm, comforting big chords from Mr. Banks.

WAY OF THE WORLD

B REAKING the tranquil mood set by 'Hold On My Heart', this swings like a big jazz band, with a clipped, snappy beat. Once again the lyricist comes up with a phrase that sounds just right for chanting to mass audiences on some starry night in a stadium: "Should the blue sky meet the red sky?" This time Genesis contemplates the conundrums faced by Man on the Planet, battling to make sense of himself and the laws of nature.

SINCE I LOST YOU

A DRAMATIC roll on the drums heralds Phil's entry on a slow, majestic processional piece, that sounds like suitable music for a Coronation: "My heart has broken into pieces since you've been gone," he warbles, with the anguish known only to those who have been in love and lost their loved one. It's enough to make strong men weep.

FADING LIGHTS

A ND SO the album draws to a close, and there are no more 'Jesus He Knows Me' jamborees, only a gentle, lulling, mellifluous slow descent into silence. The lyrics ponder on the course of personal history and what might have been – "If only we could do it all again." But as Collins, Rutherford and Banks look back, it seems "It's just another fading memory." Whether this is a requiem for passing life in general or the life of a band, it is up to the individual decide. A pattering rhythm barely disturbs the breathless air, and sustained chords hold onto the fading light for the final fleeting moments... until Genesis bid us adieu.

Calling All Stations

UK issue: Virgin GEN CD6, Released 1997.

WHEN **GENESIS WELCOMED SCOTS BORN SINGER RAY WILSON AS** their new member in 1997, it seemed like history repeating itself. The band had survived potentially fatal blows in the past. Although not entirely unexpected, given the increasing demands of his solo career, it was still a shock when Phil Collins decided to follow in the footsteps of predecessor Peter Gabriel and quit. His departure effectively robbed Genesis of its superstar lead singer, composer and drummer. Although Collins had joined when the band was already established, his contribution over the years had been vast. It would be a tough job for anyone to try and follow him.

Ray Wilson was a brave man and a good singer, who promised he could handle the band's massive repertoire as well as contribute towards writing some of the new material. This was evident on *Calling All Stations* the first Genesis studio album since 1991's *We Can't Dance* and the first since Phil Collins's departure in 1996. The pressure on both band and their newest recruit was immense and expectations were high. Tony Banks and Mike Rutherford wrote most of the songs, although Wilson contributed towards three of them. The aim was to produce an album that would adopt a rather more serious stance and would hopefully appeal to Genesis fans as well as uncommitted record buyers. The result was a dark, sombre album that attempted to recapitulate many of the band's most familiar characteristics, including Gabriel-esque vocals and a heavy Collins drum beat.

Wilson, the 28-year-old former lead singer with Stiltskin, had previously enjoyed a (1994) number one hit single with a song called 'Inside'. Even so, some thought him a surprising choice for Genesis. Tony Banks was reassured when he first heard Wilson try out 'No Son Of Mine'. Said Tony: "It sent shivers down my back. It was like hearing the song for the first time again." Both Mike and Tony enjoyed what they called the 'natural darkness' in Ray's voice. It was also their intention to bring back "some of the old drama" to their music.

Calling All Stations comprises 70 minutes of music spread over eleven tracks, several them eight minutes long. They were recorded at The Farm, the band's Surrey studio and were produced by Nick Davis, Banks and Rutherford. Most of the material was written before Ray Wilson was introduced to the band. The fact that the band was momentarily reduced in numbers meant that Mike in particular had to work hard during the sessions, bringing out his acoustic guitars as well as playing lead. He even re-introduced the bass pedals, a device he first used on stage in the Seventies. The band recruited percussionist Nir Zidkyahu to replaced Collins, who shared duties with American drummer Nick D'Virgilio.

The album was released in September 1997 together with a single version of the second track 'Congo'. They realised it would be difficult to relaunch themselves without the familiar face of Phil at the helm but were confident they could deliver some interesting new goods. The songs had come together quickly and Genesis ended up leaving off four or five strong tracks and a further half dozen tunes. They hoped that the public would give the album a fair hearing and appreciate the care and work that had gone into creating the longer pieces of work. More singles were released including 'Shipwrecked' and 'Not About Us'. However, neither singles nor album proved big hits.

Whereas for the previous 30 years each new Genesis album had sold more than the previous one, *Calling All Stations* achieved around 90,000 US sales. As a result a proposed American tour was cancelled. Wilson toured Europe with the band in 1998, but was disappointed when in the year 2000 it was decided that Genesis would no longer continue recording and touring. In their wake tribute bands and compilation albums have kept Genesis music alive and after a period of personal recovery, Ray Wilson began to rebuild his solo career.

CALLING ALL STATIONS

A GRINDING guitar riff and a solid backbeat sets up the all important debut track for the new look Genesis. Ray Wilson's vocal style is relatively laid back here although he employs a Celtic lilt somewhat akin to the late Phil Lynott of Thin Lizzy or U2's Bono as he builds towards a climax. The drums, (whether machine tooled or hand-crafted) tend to thud rather than swing. Bluesy guitar helps lifts the piece onto a higher plane. In the lyrics Ray cries out "Can anybody tell me, exactly where I am?" He describes losing all sense of direction while "Watching the darkness closing around me." An air of powerful menace pervades a piece that has a pessimistic yet defiant tone.

CONGO

A STRONG African rhythm builds up over the initial background of tribal shouting and hollering. Once again the dark side of Wilson's voice is heard as he intones "Send me to the Congo, I'm free to leave... just do as you please." Fuzz tone guitar hums over a sturdy if uninspiring drum track while the piece builds towards a stately conclusion interspersed with chirpy chords from Mike and Tony. All this has overtones of the band's hit sound carefully fashioned during the high tech Eighties, but without the bite, 'Congo' lacks a clear enough message.

SHIPWRECKED

A SAD BUT uplifting ballad about the miseries endured after being cast adrift in an unfulfilled relationship. The crackling sound of a radio set tuned in search of emergency signals gives way to a haunting lyric that Wilson interprets with taste and discretion. Even though the song lacks a satisfying resolution the singer creates a seascape of emotions. "I might as well be shipwrecked" mourns Ray, regretting a harsh exchange of hurtful words. He drifts and bobs like a message in a bottle floating towards a lonely shore. A clever production device is used to allow distant music to be overshot by a sudden proximity shell of exploding drums and guitar.

ALIEN AFTERNOON

O NE OF the album's most intriguing and longer pieces, 'Alien Afternoon' creates an attractively mysterious mood. It's about a man getting out of bed intending to explore the world, only to wish he were transported back home to safety and security. "I hear voices but there's nobody there" says the singer facing an alien world of confusion. A choppy, funky riff shows that Genesis can get into an R&B groove when they feel the urge. Shimmering ethereal chords from Tony Banks suspends all the protagonists in some fifth dimension of space and time.

NOT ABOUT US

A TTRACTIVELY simple acoustic guitar encourages Ray to sing more about loneliness and the need for understanding. "A little piece of something falling gently down... no one understands you like I do – it's not about us anymore," are some of the affecting, heartfelt lines that blend sympathy with sincerity.

The theme is adult, mature and decidedly hypnotic in a late Nineties way. "It's not about anger it's more about the loneliness we feel," explains Ray carefully stepping on emotional eggshells. Once the process of making past comparisons is set aside this is the sort of writing and crafted performance that repays repeated listening. 'Not About Us' deserved to be a hit single although the fade out ending proves a let down.

IF THAT'S WHAT YOU NEED

THE DESPAIRING mood is maintained on a slow paced melody that benefits from Banks' lush and romantic keyboards. "Why do I find it so difficult to let my feelings unfold," sings Ray, promising to protect his loved one. Despite the careful construction and painstaking efforts to create an epic, somehow the piece drifts into a trance that must surely leave the object of such lamentation comatose. While any gentle woman would appreciate such caring thoughts as "I'll be the river, I'll be the mountain always beside you", one can't help but suspect the modern Miss would prefer a night of merry making on the Costa del Sol with a tattooed binge drinker.

THE DIVIDING LINE

AN EXUBERANT Bo Diddley style beat lifts the all-pervading despair created by the preceding hymns to darkness. This eight-minute epic gives the drummer a chance to rock out during the lengthy introduction before the vocals re-appear. However Wilson seems to be singing in the same key and tempo as before, still plunged in gloom despite the musical fireworks going off all around. Curiously this recalls Peter Gabriel's similarly dramatic technique when narrating such early epics as 'The Knife'. Ray dutifully intones such questioning lines as "When darkness covers the city and the streets are silent too, what will you turn to?" The bands roars back with an instrumental crescendo devised with concert performance in mind.

UNCERTAIN WEATHER

THE CAPTIVATING charm of wartime photographs of long forgotten souls provides the theme for this drawn out ensemble piece in which singer and band interact with orchestral grandeur. Wilson gazes at a faded picture of "a sinner, a saint, a soldier caught up in a war" and muses on how little trace is left of the man and his hopes, dreams and schemes. Who was he? Did he have a family? We are left wondering as "Leaving no trace, disappearing like smoke in the wind" our old soldier fades away.

SMALL TALK

'Small Talk' hits a groove with a crisp backbeat although the talk is still of regret and damaged relationships. This time betrayal is the bitter cause of angry recrimination. "Don't talk back to me" snaps the singer. "Isn't it a shame you were lying to me when you said to me I was the only one." This is the somewhat bitter riposte to the woman who seems to be intent on causing trouble throughout the album. The suspicion that she really did go off to Spain with a boozy paramour can only increase as Ray grumbles above the chatter at a swish party – "How much goes on inside your head I often wonder". Violent guitar and keyboard riffs snap to a fusillade from the drummer as affections are trampled underfoot.

THERE MUST BE SOME OTHER WAY

DOOMY chords and mysterious percussion effects as it swims into a tale of woe that becomes quite heavy going. Then a ray of hope. Our bruised and battered balladeer cries out: "You're no longer part of my life." As he takes a reality check he announces to anyone who will listen "There must be some other way!" Clearly the realisation has dawned that the female who has caused him so much angst cannot be trusted and is better off sipping Sangria in the sun with her pals. You can almost hear Ray shout "Get thee to a nunnery." As his mood brightens so the band work even harder to support his emotional rescue plan.

ONE MAN'S FOOL

AN EERILY prescient song about the horrors of violent action against civil society. "As the buildings crumble, tumble to the ground and the dust filled smoke rises in the air, you know that somebody, somewhere looks with pride, they're satisfied." In his tightly controlled anger and bewilderment Ray states "Drawing lines upon the sand...then dying to defend them seems quite meaningless to me...and when the war is won will there be peace for evermore?" The problem of irresolvable differences brings 'Calling All Stations' to an angry, almost militant conclusion. There is much to savour on an album that kept the Genesis flag flying during a difficult period. At least the band had made a worthwhile artistic statement and the songs, like many of the their past efforts seems to improve with age like fine wine.

LIVE ALBUMS
Genesis Live

Original UK issue: Charisma Records CLASS 1, released July 1973;
re-issued on Charisma CLACD 1 October 1985. US Charisma CAS 1666.
Definitive Edition Remaster Virgin CLACDX 1, summer 1994

THE BAND'S FIRST LIVE ALBUM WAS ORIGINALLY RECORDED BY THE US *King Biscuit Hour Show* at the De Montfort Hall, Leicester and Free Trade Hall, Manchester during February 1973. The tapes were mixed at Island Studios, London, and the album was co-produced by John Burns and Genesis. Although the band hadn't intended to release a live album, the tapes, intended originally for American radio, were so good Charisma felt they should be heard on record. The result was an invaluable souvenir of a time when the band were playing at their best to wildly appreciative audiences. *Foxtrot* had eventually got into the charts after a long struggle and the band were playing to bigger crowds.

Says Tony Banks: "This was never intended to be a live album and we said we really didn't want one out, as it was too soon. Then the record company said they wanted to put it out in Germany and we agreed, being pretty naive. So then they said they had to put it out in England or there would be trouble with imported copies. Then we had to put it out everywhere!"

Often fond memories of great concerts by legendary bands are ruined when many years later the awful evidence of live tapes emerges. In the case of Genesis this example of the band in concert simply proves they more than justified their reputation for excellence. The complex arrangements, so familiar from the studio albums, take on a new lease of live when performed in front of an adoring, receptive audience. The band were honed by the nightly grind of touring, and even if there were better concerts, the show captured here remains a wonderful example of their art.

WATCHER OF THE SKIES

THE ECHO in the concert hall only adds to the atmosphere and enhances the roaring mystical power of the Mellotron as Tony Banks sets up the band's most urgent and menacing *tour de force*. You can hear the sharp crack of Phil Collins' snare drum as he builds up the pressure. All the instruments, notably the bass guitar and bass pedals have a stronger presence than on the studio recordings, and the clarity of the uncluttered mix is actually far superior. You can even hear the tambourine. Phil sings back-up from the drum kit, something most spectators missed at concerts as the spotlight was invariably on Peter. The band prove they can recreate everything that was done on the original versions, with added zest and confidence. The soft-loud passages are brilliantly done before the final blitzkrieg, as Phil ends his tom tom roll, just a fraction of a second too soon.

GET 'EM OUT BY FRIDAY

PETER raises a laugh from fans, simply by muttering "Good evening". The drums kick and the band positively swing with such commanding power you just wish you could go down the road to the Marquee Club and see this version of the band, reunited and playing live tonight. This version comes complete with the bizarre voice of Genetic Control.

THE RETURN OF THE GIANT HOGWEED

PHIL COUNTS in the tempo from his bass drum and the guitar and organ launch into the swirling, rotary pattern of the main theme in tight unison. Peter sings of the Victorian explorer who brings home to Engand the giant weed that would prove such a curse, while the band revel in the chance to play at full bore. Collins' ensemble playing here is superb as the massed ranks of Genesis collide amidst some huge, fat chords, blasting and slashing in the final struggle to overcome the voracious weeds.

THE MUSICAL BOX

AS DESULTORY notes are heard from the depths of the band, Gabriel announces in his clipped British tones: "That was an unaccompanied bass pedal solo by Michael Rutherford". It was a shame that Peter's longer stories and chats with the audience were not included on the album, but with such a huge amount of music to get through, there was no space for Gabriel's entertaining banter.

The recording quality is so good, you can clearly hear Phil's cymbals picking out the melody as Hackett and Rutherford state the theme, while the toms roar with a depth then unattainable in the studio. As the band rush towards a kind of nirvana, creating a great orchestral hymn in the process, Peter yells 'Now!" and the audience feels hair rising on the backs of their necks,

THE KNIFE

"The Knife" calls out a voice from the audience. "The Knife" answers Peter coolly.

Marching into this most violent and psychotic of Genesis works, Gabriel bellows: "Stand up and fight, for you know we are right," which signals the band's exceptional use of disciplined team work. During the quieter moments, the flute is used most effectively, then Hackett takes over, given more space for expression than usual. The bolero rhythm which takes us to the finale is so exciting the band almost – but not quite – slips out of control.

Seconds Out

Original UK issue: Charisma GE 2001, released October 1977;
re-issued Charisma GECD 2001 April 1992. US Atlantic SD2 9002.
Definitive Edition Remaster, Virgin GECDX 2001 Autumn 1994.

THEIR FIRST FULLY APPROVED LIVE ALBUM, RECORDED IN PARIS DURING 1976/77 with the Manor Mobile studio and mixed at Trident Studios, London. The double LP set, illustrated with pictures by their devoted photographer and biographer Armando Gallo, celebrated the transition of Genesis from cult band to mega rock attraction. They had a new manager, Tony Smith (not to be confused with the late Tony Stratton-Smith), who had taken over during 1974, and employed an ever expanding crew of light and sound technicians.

There were 12 tracks covering a spectrum of past Genesis material including the more recent 'Squonk', 'Firth Of Fifth' and 'Dance On A Volcano'. There was also a marathon version of 'Supper's Ready', which covered the whole of side three of the original vinyl album. While most of the drumming chores were split between Phil Collins and Chester Thompson, Bill Bruford's stay in the band was recalled with his contribution to 'Cinema Show'. Phil was also featured on keyboards, notably on 'Robbery, Assault & Battery' and 'Cinema Show'. The album also marked the last appearance of guitarist Steve Hackett before his departure to pursue a solo career. The band had planned a double live album for some time and recorded one of their tours with Bill Bruford. Then Chester Thompson joined and his contribution was recorded in Paris. When it came to mixing, producer David Hentschel and the band decided that the combination of Chester and Phil's drumming worked better and the Bruford tapes were dropped. While the tracks were being mixed, Steve Hackett announced he wanted to quit.

Remembers Tony Banks. "Steve left in the middle of it. Phil saw him in the street and asked if he wanted a lift to the studio, and he just said: 'Oh no, I'll see you later.' Later on he rang up and said he wasn't coming back! It was nice to include 'Supper's Ready' on the live album. It sounds much better than the original."

SQUONK

CULLED from *A Trick Of The Tail*, the first post-Gabriel album, it introduces us to a new age of Genesis, armed with Chester Thompson on drums. Here is a band transformed into a rock institution after eight years of writing, recording and touring. They sound cool, assured and workmanlike. This tearful tale is boosted by an insistent, measured beat behind Phil's somewhat distant vocals.

THE CARPET CRAWL

AN EXTREMELY soft and subtle performance of the piece originally called 'The Carpet Crawlers' on *The Lamb*. "You've got to get in, to get out," sings Collins gently, while Thompson sustains a constant hi-hat rhythm. It's likely some extra effects were dubbed on at the mixing stage. Certainly, there is an eerie precision about some of the playing, that you might not expect to find in a live situation, but the applause sounds real.

ROBBERY, ASSAULT & BATTERY

TO WAKE up the audience, the band embark on a jaunty saga first heard on *A Trick Of The Tail*. The crowd clap along to the beat, but one wonders how many of the French audience could actually understand Collins' Cockney spiel. The quirky keyboard solo is all Phil, and the chirpy melody is carefully sandwiched in the band's set between two rather serious, subdued pieces.

AFTERGLOW

A HIGHLIGHT of the *Wind & Wuthering* album, this has a restrained, swaying rhythm, with Phil singing in his most restrained and sensitive fashion. The melody is one that grows and glows with an inner warmth, while the choral backing, courtesy of Banks' marvellous machines, is very attractive. During the big build up, Phil joins Chester in the drum drama.

FIRTH OF FIFTH

FOR THE first time during this album Steve Hackett's guitar is detectable as he plays some desultory figures over Tony Banks' rippling, swirling cascade of keyboard notes. The drums are clipped and restless on a routine instrumental performance of the work first heard on *Selling England By The Pound*. Phil sings with all his West London roots showing as he warbles of "The riva of constant change!"

I KNOW WHAT I LIKE

Phil's 'scat' singing is one of the highlights of this extended version of their early hit song. He also does his tambourine routine, in which he used to beat himself practically senseless on the head, drawing roars of applause. This is rather like listening to a football match on the radio – without a commentator. The piece actually starts to fall asleep during a long, coasting instrumental section, but wakes up on its return to the theme. Mike Rutherford's nifty bass patterns provide some of the most interesting moments.

THE LAMB LIES DOWN ON BROADWAY

A section from the major work that was one of The Lamb's more memorable themes and works well taken out of context. The audience clap along, out of time, the sort of thing that drives most drummers to distraction. Despite the enthusiasm of the French fans, there remains a strangely listless feel about the music. Whether this was due to the flat recording sound, lack of inspiration on the night, Steve Hackett's diminished role, or the recent switch of drummers, which entailed Chester Thompson learning a huge library of

unfamiliar music, is hard to determine.

THE MUSICAL BOX

Amazingly, with just a brief snatch of the old faithful 'Musical Box', the band suddenly catches fire. It's great to hear the organ roar as Phil yells "Touch me!" and then launches into frenzied cries of "Now, now, now!" The drums cut loose, and Hackett's all important guitar phrases bring the piece to a crashing climax greeted with wild cheers and chants.

SUPPER'S READY

Although held to be a better recording than the original, this is an oddly flat version of the Foxtrot album classic. Phil does his best, but he isn't Peter Gabriel, and Peter's manic intensity and propensity for the bizarre is sorely missed, especially from sections like 'Willow Farm'. You can't imagine Phil as a flower somehow. There is some good playing of course, notably from Tony Banks who offers dynamic organ work, and 'Apocalypse In 9/8' is brightened by snare drum exchanges from Collins and Thompson. But there is no guts to the performance, and when Phil isn't on the drums, Chester sounds lost. There isn't enough guitar to add electrostatic crackle, and 'Supper's Ready' sounds microwaved rather than oven cooked.

CINEMA SHOW

IF THE band's heart wasn't really into playing 'Supper's Ready' for the umpteenth time during these French shows, they certainly seemed more inspired while playing more recent material. Acoustic guitars tremble before Phil sings in the upper register about Romeo and Juliet off to the pictures. The guitar emulates the sound of trickling water and seagulls and it was quite daring to sustain long periods of nothing but sound effects. Today's impatient audiences, with a lower attention span, might respond to this by hurling beer cans and firecrackers. Instead the Genesis buffs of the Seventies listen enthralled, and are rewarded by the band suddenly waking up to launch into a clipped, staccato section. Here Bill Bruford makes his presence felt with some superb drumming. His tom-toms roar and the snare drum and hi-hats skitter around the beat. When Phil and Bill join forces for the climax after a lengthy instrumental work out, they create some of the most exciting and spontaneous moments of the double album.

DANCE ON A VOLCANO/ LOS ENDOS

THE FIRST and last tracks from *A Trick Of The Tail* are merged into one spirited show stopper. Phil sings a haunting refrain until Chester Thompson joins him in a lively drum duet. There is much more fire in their playing here than is evident on some of the other 'live' material. As the guitar and keyboards wail, you can imagine the audience holding up their blazing cigarette lighters in supplication and shouting out in heavy French accents, "Phil-eep!" What we actually hear is a recording of Ethel Merman singing 'There's No Business Like Show Business.'

Three Sides Live

Original UK issue: Charisma Double LP GE 2002, released June 1982;
US; Atlantic SD 2-2000, June 1982.
Re-issued on Charisma GECD 2002, April 1992.

The American and British versions of this double package vary considerably. Most of the material was recorded live in Europe and American during 1981, although 'Watcher Of The Skies', on the fourth side of the UK release, came from a 1976 concert. On side four of the US version of the original vinyl LP the record company included 'Paperlate', 'You Might Recall' and 'Me And Virgil'. These three were held back from *Abacab* and put on a British Extended Play (EP) disc. The US album also had other two songs, 'Evidence Of Autumn' and 'Open Door'.

Says Tony Banks: "We had a lot of songs which weren't on the previous live album, so it seemed about time to do another one. There isn't a lot to say about it really except that on the American version we decided to use the spare tracks from *Abacab* plus a couple of spare ones from *Duke* to make up the fourth side, which was why we called it *Three Sides Live*. Songs like 'One For The Vine' which we put on the British version had never been very popular in America and we felt it wasn't right to put them on the US album. We could also call the British LP *Three Sides Live* because there were three of us!"

TURN IT ON AGAIN

GENESIS in full cry with their revamped touring band, augmented by long stay American friends Chester Thompson (drums) and Daryl Stuermer (guitar). The set featured a mix of songs drawn from then current albums like *Duke* and *Abacab*, with nods in the direction of Wind And Wuthering, *The Lamb* and *Foxtrot*. 'Turn It On Again' from 1980's *Duke* has a pounding Indian war chant rhythm greeted by cheers from the crowds milling about beyond the footlights. Phil sings with great humour and skill, cleverly using echo to emphasise key phrases. He shows complete mastery over both audience and song. His cry of "Turn it on again!" becomes a jazz scat vocal as he tortures and toys with the words. He obviously has much more fun with the newer material than standard, early Genesis fare.

DODO

CHESTER Thompson shouts out the count for the grinding riff from the 1981 *Abacab* album. Collins introduces the growling cry of "Ow!" that he developed a few years later to become the focal point of 'Mama' on the Genesis album. During this period we can hear Phil make a great vocal leap forward from his more mournful Seventies period. He sounds bolder, more inventive, and frequently uses his voice like another musical instrument on this untypical Genesis performance. This is music beyond category, that combines all the band's past experience and influences.

ABACAB

MORE CLICKS from the sticks as the band zooms straight into the staccato rhythm that characterises the piece. Thumping bass drums double up the beat, and there's a touch of *The Twilight Zone* from Tony Banks before the bass guitar locks into a single note pulse broken up by crashing cymbals. This is jazz, rock, classical and funk music all compressed and distilled into a strange and highly potent blend. The 'live' sound is extraordinary. This was either a road crew's PA heaven, or there was a lot of post production re-mixing.

BEHIND THE LINES

ANOTHER song from *Duke*. Loud huzzahs greet the broadside of exultant chords as the band take off on some grand musical odyssey. As the tempo accelerates you can hear every note from the bell of the cymbals, every instrument of the Genesis orchestra clearly defined in the mix. Phil sings with a hint of Tamla Motown as he emerges from his beloved drum kit to hit centre stage.

DUCHESS

A GENTLE drum machine rhythm is joined by various percussion effects, setting up the mood for Phil to sing about his mysterious 'Duchess' (the second track on *Duke*).

In the early days of new music technology some die-hards were shocked that a top drummer like Collins would use a machine, especially on stage. However, it was the way new Genesis songs were being constructed, and it all made sense in that context.

ME & SARAH JANE

DRUM machines return, giving a strict tempo which profoundly affected all pop and rock henceforth. Special emphasis on a metronomic beat gave Genesis songs more discipline although the band could still switch moods and rhythms at the drop of a tambourine, or the press of a button. This develops into a strange pastiche of Madness-style ska. Well played, but in Genesis terms, very peculiar.

FOLLOW YOU, FOLLOW ME

B RIGHT and bouncy with jaunty synthesiser from Banks on one of those simple pop songs that Genesis do so well. Phil sounds a tad breathless, unusually so for a man who normally displays inexhaustible supplies of energy. He'd probably just completed a twenty minute drum solo, a tap dance routine and the whole of 'Supper's Ready', minutes before singing this particular item.

MISUNDERSTANDING

"YOU LEFT me in the rain for hours... you could have called to let me know." Sounding hurt and injured, Phil sings from the heart one of the best songs from *Duke* conceived in the days before mobile phones became widespread. Once again he shows you can't beat a simple, direct and uncomplicated lyric. The band lock into a great swinging groove over an irresistible beat and the whole piece turns into a real Blues Brothers romp. The abrupt, unexpected ending is a treat.

IN THE CAGE

"I GOT sunshine in my stomach," sings Collins in an an extract from the Lamb. While containing some of the better instrumental bits from the double album, the lyrics had begun to sound dated, even by 1981. The band plunge into 'Cinema Show' from *Selling England By The Pound* and then *The Lamb*'s 'Slippermen', as part of a medley which gives Tony Banks plenty of freedom of movement during a keyboard *tour de force*. Collins and Thompson alternate stereo enhanced snare drum 'fills' in a fevered climax.

AFTERGLOW

A BEAUTIFUL treatment of the song from Wind And Wuthering, on which Phil sings sadly "For now I have lost everything" with his usual knack for unpretentious conviction. Ironically he was in the throes of gaining everything at the time, as his solo career sky rocketed with the release of 'In The Air Tonight' and *Face Value*. However, this is a splendid performance, marred only by a slight cock up in the drum department in the final bars.

ONE FOR THE VINE

A DELICATE interpretation of another *Wind And Wuthering* song recorded during a 1980 concert. You could hear a pin drop during this pretty, subdued piece, until Tony Banks seizes his grand piano by the throat and goes for broke. Few would actually dare to drop pins while the maestro was in action.

FOUNTAIN OF SALMACIS

P HIL REVIVES Peter Gabriel's original vocal style on a piece culled from 1971's *Nursery Cryme*, the first Genesis album on which Collins appeared. Workmanlike rather than atmospheric, the band sound as if they are going through the motions.

IT/WATCHER OF THE SKIES

T HE AUDIENCE claps vigorously on an inappropriate beat while Phil sings the final item from the original Lamb album, concluding with the famous line: "It's only knock and knowall, but I like it." Phil concludes this historic item with a hasty: "Thank you, see ya!" Much better is a powerful and welcome revival of 'Watcher Of The Skies' from 1972's superb *Foxtrot* album.

It's a good opportunity to hear Bill Bruford and Phil go berserk during this brief extract from a 1976 concert recording that concludes with thunderous, menacing chords. You can imagine the band rushing back to the dressing room for hot towels and brandy as the happy, excited audience files out in search of the nearest chip shop and bus queue, or burgers and Yellow cabs if they are young Americans. "Did you see that dude Phil Collins play tambourine? Awesome!"

The Way We Walk

Genesis Live

Volume One: The Shorts

UK issue: Virgin GEN CD 4, November 1992

IN 1992 GENESIS SET OFF ON THEIR EAGERLY AWAITED WORLD TOUR which included extensive gigging in the United States and Europe.

The show featured a remarkable new stage set, involving a specially low slung rig which gave the impression the band were performing under a tubular steel proscenium arch. The shows were recorded for posterity and later released in two volumes. The quality, as one might expect from Genesis in the Nineties was excellent, and shows how the standards achieved on the *Invisible Touch*, and *We Can't Dance* albums were maintained in a live situation on stage. The first volume of live recordings included the best of the band's contemporary hits. One notable difference between these, and the band's previous live recordings is the sound of the audience, who are much more demonstrative.

TRACKS: Land Of Confusion/No Son Of Mine/Jesus He Knows Me/ Throwing It All Away/ I Can't Dance/Mama/Hold On My Heart/That's All/ In Too Deep/Tonight, Tonight, Tonight/Invisible Touch

The Way We Walk

Genesis Live

Volume Two: The Longs

UK issue: Virgin GENCD, January 1993

THE SECOND VOLUME OF LIVE PERFORMANCES FEATURED LENGTHY VERSIONS of the band's epic material culled from various eras in their career.

It opened with brief excerpts from four old favourites compressed into a medley, and concluded with an exciting drum duet featuring Phil Collins and Chester Thompson. The band's line up on the tour included Phil (vocals, drums) with Tony Banks (keyboards, vocals), Mike Rutherford (guitar, bass & vocals), Daryl Stuermer (guitar, bass, & vocals), and Chester Thompson (drums).

The playing is immaculate throughout and is notable for Daryl and Mike's guitar playing, more heavily featured than usual on record.

TRACKS: Dance On A Volcano/Lamb Lies Down On Broadway/The Musical Box/Firth Of Fifth (Medley)/I Know What I Like/Driving The Last Spike/Domino Part 1 – In The Glow Of The Night/Part 2 – The Last Domino/Fading Lights/Home By The Sea/Drum Duet

COMPILATION ALBUMS

Genesis:
The Invisible Series

UK issue: Boxed set Virgin GENDX 9, 1992

THIS ATTRACTIVELY PACKAGED BOXED SET WAS TIMED TO COINCIDE WITH the band's British dates in the summer of 1992, which included concerts at Roundhay Park, Leeds (July 31) and Knebworth Park (August 1 & 2). The box includes five CD singles' worth of tracks culled from the *We Can't Dance* album with previously unreleased live tracks. One of them, 'Land Of Confusion' on Volume 5 of the set was recorded during rehearsals for the *We Can't Dance* World Tour of 1992. The artist Felicity Roma Bowers, whose work graced the *We Can't Dance* CD, illustrated the whole package. Volume 2 includes a brief band chronology and discography as well as bonus track 'On The Shoreline.' Volume 4 of the series includes a set of Genesis postcards.

VOLUME ONE: NO SON OF MINE Virgin GENDG 6
No Son Of Mine/Living Forever/Invisible Touch (Live)

VOLUME TWO: I CAN'T DANCE Virgin GENDG 7
I Can't Dance/On The Shoreline/ In Too Deep (Live)/That's All (Live)

VOLUME THREE: HOLD ON MY HEART Virgin GENSD 8
Hold On My Heart/ Way Of The World/Home By The Sea (Live)

VOLUME FOUR: HOLD ON MY HEART Virgin GENDG 8
Hold On My Heart/Way Of The World/Your Own Special Way (Live)

VOLUME FIVE: JESUS HE KNOWS ME Virgin GENDX 9
Jesus He Knows Me/Hearts On Fire/Land Of Confusion (Rehearsal Version)

Genesis Archive 1967-75

UK issue: 4-CD Box Set, Virgin 72458 42221 23;
US Atlantic 82858, June 1998

THIS FASCINATING FOUR-CD BOXED SET PRESENTS FANS WITH THE opportunity to hear a complete live recording of *The Lamb Lies Down On Broadway* performed at The Shrine Auditorium, Los Angeles in 1975, which sheds new light on the band's most controversial epic. Amidst the cries of "Peter!" the singer announces they have a "big lump of story and music" and outlines the adventures of 'Rael' before Tony Banks launches into a mesmeric piano introduction. The wild enthusiasm of an attentive audience shows the strength of the band's dedicated American following.

Two CDs are devoted to *The Lamb*, performed with greater power and enthusiasm than the studio version. CDs 3 and 4 include more live recordings from 1973's Rainbow Theatre, London concert as well as BBC broadcasts and demos. The slipcase has an 82-page booklet containing essays and interviews with Tony Banks, Jonathan King, Chris Welch and other Genesis associates.

DISC 1: The Lamb Lies Down On Broadway, Fly On A Windshield, Broadway Melody Of 1974, Cuckoo Cocoon, In The Cage, The Grand Parade Of Lifeless Packaging, Back In N.Y.C., Hairless Heart, Counting Out Time, Carpet Crawlers, The Chamber Of 32 Doors

DISC 2: Lilywhite Lilith, The Waiting Room, Anyway, Here Comes The Supernatural Anaesthetist, The Lamia, Silent Sorrow In Empty Boats, The Colony Of Slippermen (The Arrival, A Visit To The Doktor, The Raven), Ravine, The Light Dies Down On Broadway, Riding The Scree, In The Rapids, it

DISC 3 (L = LIVE): Dancing with the Moonlight Knight (L), Firth of Fifth (L), More Fool Me (L), Suppers Ready (L), I Know What I Like (L), Stagnation (L), Twilight Alehouse, Happy The Man, Watcher Of The Skies

DISC 4: In The Wilderness, Shepherd, Pacidy, Let Us Now Make Love, Going Out To Get You, Dusk, Build Me A Mountain, Image Blown Out, One Day, Where The Sour Turns To Sweet, In The Beginning, The Magic Of Time, Hey!, Hidden in the World Of Dawn, Sea Bee, The Mystery Of The Flannan Isle Lighthouse, Hair On The Arms And Legs, She Is Beautiful, Try A Little Sadness, Patricia

---

Turn It On Again :
The Hits

UK issue: Virgin GENCDX8 October 1999;
US Atlantic 83244, October 1999

THE SONG WRITING TEAM OF BANKS, RUTHERFORD AND COLLINS WENT INTO overdrive during the latter part of their careers together, producing a string of vibrant pop hits that introduced a whole new generation to a band that was already legendary. Even if their new fans weren't privy to the delights of their early days, when they were playing 'Watcher Of The Skies' in small clubs, they were privileged to hear such joyful and evocative pieces as 'Invisible Touch' and 'Land Of Confusion'. These are great songs by any standards. This satisfying collection celebrates the band's Golden Age of chart success.

TRACKS: Turn It On Again, Invisible Touch, Mama, Land Of Confusion, I Can't Dance, Follow You Follow Me, Hold On My Heart, Abacab, I Know What I Like, No Son Of Mine, Tonight Tonight Tonight, In Too Deep, Congo, Jesus He Knows Me, That's All, Misunderstanding, Throwing It All Away, The Carpet Crawlers, 1999

Genesis Archive
1976-1992

UK issue: Virgin CDBOX7, November 2000;
Atlantic 83410, November 2000

THE SECOND VOLUME OF GENESIS ARCHIVE MATERIAL PROBES INTO THE more commercially successful Phil Collins era from 1976 until his departure in the mid-Nineties. This three CD box set includes rarities, B-sides, 12 inch mixes and outstanding live versions of such songs as 'Your Own Special Way' and 'Duke's Travels'. There is also a glimpse of the band putting their dynamic hit 'Mama' into shape. Most of the music has never appeared on CD before. A 64-page booklet has a foreword by Tony Banks.

DISC 1: On The Shoreline, Hearts On Fire, You Might Recall, Paperlate, Evidence Of Autumn, Do The Neurotic, I'd Rather Be You, Naminanu, Inside And Out, Feeding The Fire, I Can't Dance 12", Submarine

DISC 2: Illegal Alien (L), Dreaming While You Sleep (L), It's Gonna Get Better (L), Deep In The Motherlode (L), Ripples (L), The Brazilian (L), Your Own Special Way (L), Burning Rope (L), Entangled (L), Duke's Travels (L)

DISC 3: *Invisible Touch* 12", Land Of Confusion 12", Tonight, Tonight, Tonight 12", No Reply At All (L), Man On The Corner (L), The Lady Lies (L), Open Door, The Day The Light Went Out, Vancouver, Pigeons, It's Yourself, Mama (work in progress)

Platinum Collection

UK issue; Virgin 3-CD Box Set Virgin 7243 8 63730 21, 2004;
US Rhino 78446, March 2005

"**PLATINUM COLLECTION IS AS CLOSE AS IT GETS TO A DEFINITIVE GENESIS** album," says rock critic Hugh Fielder in his notes to this song packed 3-CD set. The first fully comprehensive compilation in the band's 30-year career, Platinum puts their changing moods and musical development into focus. Phil, Tony and Mike offer their thoughts on the 'magical chemistry' that held them all together and resulted in so much remarkable music. CD 1 concentrates on their block buster hits, while CDs 2 and 3 explore the transitional Seventies and features classics from 'Supper's Ready' to 'Abacab'.

DISC 1: No Son Of Mine, I Can't Dance, Jesus He Knows Me, Hold On My Heart, Invisible Touch, Throwing It All Away, Tonight Tonight Tonight (Edit), Land Of Confusion, In Too Deep, Mama, That's All, Home By The Sea, Second Home By The Sea, Illegal Alien, Paperlate, Calling All Stations

DISC 2: Abacab, Keep It Dark, Turn It On Again, Behind The Lines, Duchess, Misunderstanding, Many Too Many, Follow You Follow Me, Undertow, In That Quiet Earth, Afterglow, Your Own Special Way, A Trick Of The Tail, Ripples, Los Endos

DISC 3: The Lamb Lies Down On Broadway, Counting Out Time, Carpet Crawlers, Firth Of Fifth, The Cinema Show, I Know What I Like (In Your Wardrobe), Supper's Ready, The Musical Box, The Knife

Sensible pullovers amidst the marble halls. This grand setting reflected the solidity of Mike, Phil and Tony's long lasting musical achievements. *(Ebet Roberts/Redferns)*

...*And Then There Were Three*...
(1978) featured standout tracks
'Undertow', 'Follow You Follow Me'
and 'Say It's Alright Joe'. By now
Genesis' popularity and album
sales had increased throughout
the globe.

A new decade, style and sound.
Genesis greeted the Eighties with
Duke (1980). The minimalist album
cover design and brisk playing
confused some older fans, but no
one could deny stand out track,
'Turn It On Again' was an instant
Genesis classic.

Deep in the Home Counties - Mike, Phil and Tony, circa *Abacab* (1981).
(LFI)

Phil sings with gusto while Mike partners new guitarist mate Daryl
Stuermer for a round of chords. *(David Redfern/Redferns)*

All change! Released in 1981
Abacab was a UK Number One and
Genesis' first US Top Ten platinum
album. It yielded 'No Reply At All,'
featuring a funky horn section.

Three Sides Live, the double album
documenting the band's concert
work during 1981, also showed
Phil's mastery over an audience.
It followed on from the success
of *Seconds Out*, the band's
1977 live set.

'Hey Gringo!' Three dodgy Mexicans with false moustaches and large hats making a pop promo video. Mike, Phil and Tony on the set of 'Illegal Alien,' one of the hit songs from *Genesis* (1983).
(Brian Rasic/Rex Features)

Genesis saw the band reach new heights of creativity and popularity. 'Mama' with its drum machine beat and Collins' growling vocals became one of several chart hits.

Invisible Touch (1986) included an irresistible title track as well as such songs as 'Tonight, Tonight, Tonight', 'Land Of Confusion' and 'Throwing It All Away'. This was their finest commercial hour.

Once a struggling 'underground' act, by the mid-Eighties, Tony, Mike and Phil were amongst the top echelon of rock earners. *(LFI)*

'Invisible Touch' tour, Wembley, London 1987.
(Andre Csillag/Rex Features)

Tony Banks and Mike Rutherford in rehearsal. *(LFI)*

Tony, Phil and Mike pause at the mixing desk. *(Mel Yates/Retna)*

'The Shorts.' Not a reference to the band's trouser department, but the brevity of the tracks on their best selling compilation *The Way We Walk* (1992).

Older, but wiser, 1991. Is Phil Collins contemplating a career without Genesis? *(Paul Bergen/Redferns)*

'The Longs.' The companion hit compilation of 'The Way We Walk' with lengthy live versions of 'Dance On A Volcano,' 'Musical Box' et al.

Tony Banks, Ray Wilson and Mike Rutherford form the new look Genesis, 1997. *(Roy Tee/SIN/Corbis)*

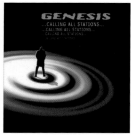

'Calling All Stations' - here is the news. Phil Collins *has* left Genesis and been replaced by Ray Wilson, formerly of Stiltskin, who makes his debut on this 1997 album.

Ray Wilson's 'dark' vocal style appealed to Tony and Mike when they sought to replace the departed Collins. Ray bravely takes the stage with the veteran band on tour in February 1998. *(Robert Eric/Corbis Sygma)*

Ray Wilson during the final Genesis tour before bowing to the inevitable.
(Robert Eric/Corbis Sygma)

SOLO ALBUMS

PETER GABRIEL

Peter Gabriel 1

UK issue: Charisma CDS 4006 released February 1977;
US Atco SD 36-147; re-issued UK Charisma CD 8000912 May 1983;
Charisma PGCD1 May 1987

WHILE MANY MOURNED THE DEPARTURE OF PETER GABRIEL FROM
Genesis, it was quickly realised, on the release of his debut solo
album, that fans would be treated to a bonus. The division of talents
resulted in a strengthening of musical output. While Genesis went on to
even greater commercial success without him, Gabriel achieved his own
artistic fulfilment and produced hit records to boot. Naturally there was
huge interest in what Peter would come up with in the wake of his much-
publicised split. He might well have been nervous. It was like starting his
career all over again. But he enjoyed a rest, recovered from the 'The Lamb
Lies Down' trauma and plunged himself into work, writing and recording
with new musicians. Some expected him to return to a kind of early
Genesis vein, with long, theatrical epics used as a peg for more costume
drama. But few really believed such a sensitive, intelligent and committed
artist would take such an option. He had plenty of new ideas – about
sound itself, the use of instruments, the way records are made, and of
course he had many new songs to play packed with the strange ideas that
haunted and obsessed him. He enthusiastically embraced and encouraged
the concept of World Music, explored darker, more cerebral themes and
utilised electronics and the avant-garde in his quest to explore different
musical avenues.

From 1977 onwards Peter released a series of solo albums, all called
Peter Gabriel. To avoid confusion, they are now usually numbered 1 to 4.
Peter Gabriel 1 was recorded in Toronto, Canada, and produced by Bob Ezrin,
who had previously worked with Alice Cooper and Kiss. The musicians he
and Gabriel gathered for the studio band included Allan Schwartzberg
(drums), Tony Levin (bass and tuba), Jim Maelem (percussion), Steve
Hunter (guitars), Robert Fripp (guitars and banjo), Jozef Chirowski
(keyboards), Larry Fast (synthesisers) and Dick Wagner (vocals, guitar).

Public and media speculation was intense, and there were sighs of relief from all who wished him well, when it became apparent that *Peter Gabriel* was a marvellous album.

'Moribund The Burgomeister', the opening track, sits easily with his old image as the creator of memorable characters. Here is a reassuring touch of old Genesis humour, with the Burgomeister offering a menacing cry of "I will find out...". Peter tears straight into 'Solsbury Hill' as if to show he hadn't lost his deft touch at creating quality pop songs. It helped re-establish Gabriel's credentials world-wide and it was a welcome boost for the album and his subsequent tour, when the single got to number 13 in the UK chart in April, 1977.

The heavy funk riff 'Modern Love' is a soulful, sexy ditty which contains the memorable line "I twisted my penis... love can be a strain". Changing the mood entirely, the lugubrious 'Excuse Me' can be interpreted as a wry commentary on his departure from Genesis. Sung by a barbershop choir, there is a touch of Randy Newman about the two beat rhythm, and humorous tuba solo, courtesy of Tony Levin. 'Humdrum' and 'Slowburn' display Gabriel's mature vocal style.

He compensates for the loss of the old Genesis 'wall of sound' by bringing on the entire London Symphony Orchestra to provide a dramatic introduction to 'Down The Dolce Vita'. This song, about a ship setting off on an epic voyage, and the moving 'Here Comes The Flood', are both linked to a theme about one of Peter's imaginary characters, Mozo, a mercurial stranger who leaves tumult and change in his wake. The same subject recurs in later albums.

Peter Gabriel 2

UK issue: Charisma CDS 4013, June 1978; US Atco SD 19181; re-issued UK Charisma PGCD, May 1987

GUITARIST **ROBERT FRIPP, LEADER OF KING CRIMSON, PRODUCED GABRIEL'S** second album, recorded at Relight Studios, Hilvarenbeek, Holland and The Hit Factory, New York. The personnel changed from the first album and included Peter (vocals, organ, piano, synth, Roy Bittan (keyboards), Jerry Marotta (drums), Tony Levin (bass), Sid McGinnis and Fripp (guitars), Larry Fast (synthesisers), Timmy Capello (sax), and George Marge (recorders).

Fripp had apparently been unhappy with Bob Ezrin's production style on the first album, and kept his involvement with Gabriel's touring band a secret, even to the extent of using a pseudonym and hiding in the wings during performances. However Gabriel had been a fan of Fripp's since the earliest days of Genesis and was anxious to work with him. Fripp's production here is looser and less pushy than Ezrin's but Atlantic record executives were somewhat displeased when they heard the results. They apparently felt the album lacked obvious hits like 'Solsbury Hill', and 'Modern Love'. This was unfair as 'D.I.Y.', a strong plea for independence and self-sufficiency, had considerable chart potential.

There is a marked difference in Peter's vocal attack on songs like 'On The Air', where he sounds mannered and influenced by American new wave. Much better is his sensitive treatment of 'Mother Of Violence', introduced by the disturbing sound of winged insects. This was co-written by Peter and his wife Jill, as a children's Christmas carol. Although the album takes time to catch fire and lacks the punch of the debut, it is packed with sensitive and imaginative performances like the exceptional 'White Shadow' and the singularly beautiful 'Indigo' where Peter sings a lament accompanied by George Marge's plaintive recorders. 'Animal Magic' is a confident, strutting rocker and a typical piece of wry humour, mocking the macho attitudes expressed in Army recruitment campaigns.

Peter Gabriel 3

UK issue: Charisma CDS 4019, June 1980; US Mercury SRM-1-3848; re-issued Charisma PGCD 3, May 1987

"**PETER DOESN'T WANT ME TO USE ANY CYMBALS!**" COMPLAINED PHIL Collins when he was invited to record with Gabriel, for the first time since *The Lamb*.

It was Peter's idea to rely on the powerful sound of the drums alone. When Phil began fooling around in the studio on his kit, producer Steve Lillywhite and engineer Hugh Padgham discovered an extraordinary effect created by a new device called a gate compressor unit. The sound Peter, Phil and the engineers heard coming through monitor headphones and over speakers in the control room was 'gated reverb', an abrupt cut off of the natural reverberation of the drum sound. Peter was so delighted by the effect he wrote a song called 'Intruder', built around the new sound, which became the first cut on his third album. Phil Collins would use the same sound on his own solo album *Face Value*, cut in the same studio, also with engineer Hugh Padgham. The effect would revolutionise drum sounds, although there was some controversy over who had originally come up with the idea.

The third album is a leap forward, more stylistically self-assured than *Gabriel 2*, and in keeping with the mood of the new decade. Lillywhite and Padgham previously worked with XTC and were young and eager to adopt new ideas, which suited Gabriel. The stark and mechanical sounding 'Intruder' emphasises the swing towards brevity and clarity, away from the muddy, busy Seventies. New technology and fresh thinking abound on *Peter Gabriel 3*, including the first ever use in a UK studio of the revolutionary Fairlight synthesiser from Australia. This samples sounds and plays them back as melodies or effects, and Peter uses it effectively in the final moments of the hypnotic and driving 'I Don't Remember'.

Gabriel welcomed some guest artists to the sessions, including Paul Weller of The Jam who plays punchy rhythm guitar on 'And Through The Wire'. Kate Bush sings on the exciting 'No Self Control' and 'Games Without Frontiers' which became Peter's first Top Ten single as a solo artist. It got to number four in the UK charts in March 1980. The jaunty humour and construction of the piece is a joy. Kate Bush contributes the sensuous hook line "Jeux sans frontiers", while Peter comes up with the memorable phrase: "Jane plays with Willy and Willy is happy again". The flow continues with 'Not One Of Us' and 'Lead A Normal Life'. According to Gabriel's biographer Spencer Bright, American record executives who heard the album at a special playback hated the crucial track 'Biko', believing that the vast American record buying public wouldn't understand a song about a South African political activist, who died in 1977. In the end Atlantic passed on the album and it was released in America on Mercury. It went on to sell more than double *Gabriel 2*, and established Peter as a major solo artist.

Peter Gabriel 4

UK issue: Charisma PGCD, September 1982; US Geffen GHS 2011; re-issued Charisma PGCD, 1986.

IN **AUTUMN 1982 PETER TOOK PART IN A ONE-OFF GENESIS REUNION SHOW,** put on to help him out after the WOMAD festival he'd staged that summer in Shepton Mallet, Somerset, ran into financial problems. Phil and Peter performed together with Mike and Tony at the Milton Keynes Bowl, playing old favourites 'Supper's Ready' and 'The Lamb Lies Down On Broadway' to a huge crowd. When Steve Hackett joined them for

'I Know What I Like' it was the first time all five members had been on stage together since Gabriel's last show with the band in 1975. WOMAD was saved and became an annual event. Alas there were no further Genesis reunions.

The same year Peter released his powerful fourth album, known as *Security* in America. Gabriel's new American record company Geffen were unhappy at calling it simply *Peter Gabriel* so they were allowed to put 'Security' stickers on the covers. Work began after a year of touring, and the album was recorded at Crescent studios in Bath. Gabriel produced the album in conjunction with David Lord.

The influence and inspiration of World Music became even more apparent on a selection of songs which blended African polyrhythms and synthesised rock backing Peter's yearning vocals. The powerful and disturbing themes dealt with personal identity and the contrast between modern isolation and communal living. Among the best cuts are 'Shock The Monkey', 'The Rhythm Of The Heat', 'San Jacinto' and 'I Have The Touch', a song about the human need for bodily contact. Other tracks included 'The Family And The Fishing Net', 'Lay Your Hands On Me', 'Wallflower' and 'Kiss Of Life'. There are no hits like 'Games Without Frontiers' but 'Shock The Monkey' got to number 29 in the US Billboard chart and MTV regularly played its effective video, which helped introduce Gabriel's work to a wider audience. The album got to number six in the UK and 28 in America.

Peter Gabriel Plays Live

UK issue: Charisma/Virgin CDPGD 100, June 1983;
US Geffen 4012-2, 1983

HIGHLIGHT OF THIS DOUBLE LIVE SET IS A VERSION OF 'SOLSBURY HILL', which peaked at 84 in the US singles chart. The album was produced at the instigation of Geffen to satisfy American Gabriel fans, with the aim of plugging the gap between studio albums and to re-introduce older songs. Gabriel beefed up the sound by dubbing studio material onto the live tracks, a time honoured process among musicians who find that the 'warts and all' philosophy of concert recording sometimes produces too many warts. The result is a dynamic and entertaining musical document of Gabriel's solo career thus far. Among the stand out cuts are 'I Don't Remember', also released as a single. The album got to number eight in the UK and 44 in America.

Birdy

UK issue Charisma/Virgin CAS 1167), March, 1985;
US Geffen GEFD-24070

SOUNDTRACK ALBUM FROM THE FILM *BIRDY* WITH MUSIC COMPOSED and performed by Gabriel and co-produced by Daniel Lanois of U2 fame. Peter wrote the music at the request of director Alan Parker, who had made *Midnight Express*, *Bugsy Malone* and *Fame*. He had previously had a difficult experience working with Pink Floyd's Roger Waters on the film version of *The Wall*. Gabriel's personality was more to his taste. Although the album didn't sell particularly well in the US it did quite well worldwide and reached number 51 in the UK chart. Songs include 'At Night', 'Floating Dogs', 'Quiet And Alone' and 'The Heat' culled from 'Rhythm Of The Heat' on Peter's fourth album.

So

UK issue; Charisma CD PGCD 5, 1986; US Geffen 24088

THE ULTIMATE GABRIEL BLOCKBUSTER THAT RESTORED HIS FORTUNES AND gave him the success he richly deserved. The songs are all tightly conceived and edited, and there is less obvious experimentation, and no freaky sounds used for their own sake. Instead all the latest technology is fully absorbed into the music.

'Sledgehammer', one of Peter's most exultant performances, is pure funk with a shouting brass section and back up vocals headed by P.P Arnold. An award winning 'Claymation' promo video accompanied the single version made by Steve Johnson, utilising clever stop-motion techniques. The record went to number four in the UK charts and the album was a number one hit. Peter had walked away from fame in Genesis, and then tried hard to avoid the tag of being 'commercial'. Now he seemed ready for the acclaim and rewards that came in the wake of So.

Quite apart from the instantly appealing 'Sledgehammer', the album is full of fine performances. 'Red Rain' has the clattering drums later utilised by Genesis on their *Invisible Touch* album, and if Peter's vocal treatment has a touch of U2 about it, then that's down to the influence of their producer Daniel Lanois. Undoubtedly the most moving performance is 'Don't Give Up', written at a time when Peter's marriage was undergoing stress. There is a heartbreaking chorus, sung by Kate Bush, whose tremulous voice and gentle compassion is enough to make the hardest souls weep. The song reached number nine in the UK chart in November 1986, and won an Ivor Novello Award. Other delicate songs also reflect Gabriel's inner tensions and fears, like 'In Your Eyes' backed by Senegalese singer Youssou N'Dour, and the dreamlike 'Mercy Street'. But Peter takes the bull by the horns on the rocking, mocking 'Big Time', on which he tells how his bank account, mouth and belly are all getting bigger in the pursuit of success. The final track 'We Do What We're Told', is a strange, inconclusive piece inspired by accounts of American experiments in which students are ordered to inflict pain on victims in a laboratory. The 'victims' are actors – feigning agony.

Peter was voted Best British Male Artist in the annual BRIT Awards in London in February 1987 and 'Sledgehammer' was voted Best Video. Earlier, the single 'Sledgehammer' went to number one in the States for a week in July 1986 and sold a million copies worldwide. The album peaked at number two in the US *Billboard* chart. 'Big Time' was also a hit and reached 13 in the UK and number eight in America in March 1987. Altogether it was a Gabriel's greatest triumph and one in the eye for the record executive who had once asked if Gabriel "had mental problems".

Shaking The Tree

UK issue Virgin PGTVD 6 November 1990; US Geffen 9 24326-2

A **TIMELY GREATEST HITS COLLECTION COMPRISING 16 MEMORABLE** tracks including: Solsbury Hill, I Don't Remember, Sledgehammer, Family Snapshot, Mercy Street, Shaking The Tree, Don't Give Up, San Jacinto, Here Comes The Flood, Red Rain, Games Without Frontiers, Shock The Monkey, I Have The Touch, Big Time, Zaar and Biko.

Us

UK issue: Virgin/Realworld PGCD 7, September 1992;
US Geffen GEFD 24473

S **OME SIX YEARS AFTER HIS CONSPICUOUS SUCCESS WITH *SO*, DURING** which he had worked on media projects for his Real World organisation and taken part in benefit tours for Amnesty International,

Gabriel returned with a spectacular touring show and a critically acclaimed new album, produced once again by Daniel Lanois. Bagpipes herald the opening cut, 'Come Talk To Me', an impassioned plea for communication and understanding. "I did not come to steal, this is all so unreal," sings Peter, with patent sincerity. *Us* is an album to which the listener must come with some sympathy and understanding. Like so much of Gabriel's work it cannot be heard or fully appreciated out of context. It was written and recorded after his 15-year marriage to wife Jill had broken up.

As he explains in his liner notes: "Most of this record is about relationships. I am dedicating it to all those who have taught me about loving and being loved." He includes among his list of loved ones, parents, wife and family. The mood of a weary regretful search for solace is continued on 'Love To Be Loved', on which Peter sings with a soft, tender touch that drifts into a dreamlike state of grace before resuming a reverie, in which he confesses: "I recognise how much I've lost but I cannot face the cost, 'cos I love to be loved." 'Blood Of Eden' is even more tragic yet strangely beautiful, with a wonderful duet between Sinéad O'Connor and producer and guitarist-turned vocalist Daniel Lanois.

The keen observer can almost sense the act of love being carried out in a moment of great tenderness when Gabriel sings "At my request you take me in..."

To provide strength and contrast Peter switches on the main pumps to unleash a jet of superheated 'Steam', one of his grooviest ventures into soul-funk. In an age of pop conformity, only Peter would have the courage to blithely pursue the path of a musical explorer, which he does with great persistence on 'Only Us', in which strange time signatures are set against floating, word-less chants. However simplicity remains a virtue, and 'Washing Of The Water' is a masterpiece of restraint. The angry 'Digging In The Dirt' depicts a bitter marital confrontation. "Don't talk back, just drive the car... shut your mouth... this time you've gone too far!" roars Peter. This is not always a Harold The Barrel full of laughs, but the mournful introspection of 'Fourteen Black Paintings', for example, is completed by the lugubrious humour of 'Kiss That Frog'. On the final track 'Secret World' Peter sings in anguished tones "I stood in this sun sheltered place until I cold see the face – behind the face".

Secret World Live

UK issue: Virgin/Real World PGDCD, August 1994;
US Geffen GEFD 2-24722

A LIVE DOUBLE CD THAT PROVIDES AN EXCELLENT SOUVENIR OF Gabriel's 1993/94 'US' World Tour. These performances were recorded at the Palasport Nuovo, Modena, Italy on November 17 and 17, 1993 and feature Peter together with guest singer Paul Cole, David Rhodes (guitar), Shankar (violin), Tony Levin (bass), Levon Minassion (doudouk) and Manu Katche (drums).

TRACK LISTING CD 1: Come Talk To Me, Steam, Across The River, Slow Marimbas, Shaking The Tree, Red Rain, Blood Of Eden, Kiss That Frog, Washing Of The Water.
CD 2: Solisbury Hill, Digging In The Dirt, Sledgehammer, Secret World, Don't Give Up, In Your Eyes.

Ovo

UK Issue Real World PGCD9 June 5, 2000

P ETER WAS COMMISSIONED TO WRITE MUSIC AND COME UP WITH IDEAS for a show to be held inside the Millennium Dome, a Government sponsored attraction built on a large vacant site in Greenwich, London and opened on New Year's Day 2000. Many considered that the show, featuring aerial trapeze artists, was one of the highlights of the year long exhibition. This album of music for the show provided a welcome souvenir of an otherwise controversial event.

Up

UK issue Realworld PGCD11, September 2002

H AILED AS A MASTERPIECE BY FANS AND CRITICS AROUND THE WORLD, the 11th Peter Gabriel studio album finally appeared after many years of work and planning. The project began in 1993 and involved far-flung recordings sessions at exotic locations in Senegal, Singapore, the French Alps and the Amazon River as well as Peter's own Real World studios. He had written some 150 compositions during this period, eventually trimmed down to a cycle of ten carefully crafted songs about birth, life and death. He explained that the album took him so long because "Old men take more time".

Many gifted musicians took part in the sessions that included guest appearances by veteran blues guitarist Peter Green and the Blind Boys Of Alabama vocalists. With a hardcore of backing musicians, notably drummers Manu Katche and Steve Gadd, Tony Levin (bass) and David Rhodes (guitar), offering firm but sympathetic support, the music ranges from tribal rhythms and rock guitar to electronic effects and tasteful acoustic piano. 'Darkness' the opening cut sets the scene with an aggressive tone, Peter singing about the "Dark shapes under me". The song's original working title was 'House In Woods' and is about the imaginings of children, who gradually learn to accept and overcome their fears. 'Growing Up' has a wailing, gurgling effect and many of the songs use water as a metaphor for Gabriel's discreet messages.

'Sky Blue' reflects Peter's early love for American blues and has welcome vocal contributions from the Blind Boys Of Alabama. In a deeper sense it is about losing ones way amidst the vastness of nature. While 'No Way Out' is funkier, the vocals remain restrained and gentle.

'I Grieve', a moving dialogue about death, has Peter reciting in regretful tones "It was all so different..." 'The Barry Williams Show' has pointed lyrics about a reality TV chat show inspired by watching *The Jerry Springer Show*. It's about the relationship between dysfunctional behaviour and mass television. It is also one of the few fast, catchy tunes on an album that could otherwise be titled *Down*. 'My Head Sounds Like That' has a John Lennon style piano theme and is attractively sombre as Peter explores the idea that the sense of hearing can be enhanced by vivid noises. "The metal jangles as the key turns" sings Peter mysteriously on the spiritual 'More Than This' about his belief that there must be more to life than the 'reality' we see in the everyday world.

The album concludes with the orchestrated 'Signal To Noise', first performed 'live' with Nusrat Fateh Ali Khan at the VH1 Honours Awards in 1996. Nusrat died before he could record the song in the studio and the vocals here are believed taken from the live recording. Peter has described him as "One of the great singers of our time." The theme here is about the need for a sense of morality and compassion. A dreamy piano-led piece called 'The Drop' perhaps the starkest performance on the album. Set on a high flying plane, the passenger looks down through the clouds and tries to image what lies beneath. Gabriel once again came up with an album that was uncompromising and experimental, although lacking in the wry humour and ribaldry that enlivened many of his past hits.

Long Walk Home

UK issue: Real World PGCG10 2002

THIS ALBUM WAS THE SOUNDTRACK FOR AUSTRALIAN MOVIE *Rabbit Proof Fence* that dealt with the travels of displaced Aboriginal children. Gabriel's mainly instrumental pieces made use of indigenous instruments such as the didgeridoo while also featuring the late Nusrat Fateh Ali Khan (vocals) and David Sancious (organ). The CD's 15 atmospheric tracks included such scene setting titles as 'Jigalong', 'Stealing The Children', 'Unlocking The Door' and 'The Tracker'.

Hit

UK issue: Real World 5952372 2-CD set 2003

THE FIRST HITS COMPILATION SINCE 1990'S *SHAKING THE TREE* THIS DOUBLE CD set comprised some 29 tracks. CD 1 has Peter's greatest hit singles and a previously unreleased radio edit of 'Blood Of Eden'. CD 2 features his best album tracks, various mixes and live performances. Critics pointed out that Gabriel's work is so diverse and idiosyncratic that it doesn't easily lend itself to the *Hits* compilation format and yet that is undoubtedly part of his charm, appeal and lasting musical value.

While track listings vary slightly in different countries the Real World version includes the following:
CD 1: Solsbury Hill, Shock The Monkey, Sledgehammer, Don't Give Up, Games Without Frontiers, Big Time, Burn You Up, Burn You Down, Growing Up, Digging In The Dirt, Blood Of Eden, More Than This, Biko, Steam, Red Rain, Here Comes The Flood.
CD 2: San Jacinto, No Self Control, Cloudless, The Rhythm Of The Heat, I Have The Touch, I Grieve, D.I.Y., A Different Drum, The Drop, The Tower That Ate People, Lovetown, Father, Son, Signal To Noise, Downside Up (live), Washing Of The Water.

PHIL COLLINS

Face Value

UK issue: Virgin 2185, February 1981; US Atlantic SD 16029;
Re-issued Virgin CDV 2185

ALL THE PENT UP ENERGY AND FRUSTRATIONS OF THE PAST WERE RIPPED aside when Phil Collins embarked on his début solo album. It was an immediate success and caused a sensation, stunning not only Genesis fans, but also Collins himself. For years he had worked hard on behalf of others. Even as the front man of Genesis he had been part of a team, and when he was involved in Brand X, the jazz-rock outfit, where he could drum with all the freedom he required, it still wasn't entirely his own band. *Face Value*, however, was Phil's baby. The songs were written during the break up of his first marriage, and 'In The Air Tonight', 'This Must Be Love', 'I Missed Again', the haunting 'You Know What I Mean' and 'If Leaving Me Is Easy' all in some way reflected his hurt and confusion. He sang with a tenderness that touched the public's sometimes-steely heart.

A new army of Collins fans was created virtually overnight by the seductive introduction to 'In The Air Tonight', with its gentle build-up over a slow paced drum machine pattern. Phil's voice sustains the tension with minimal support until drums crash in and a torrent of passion is unleashed. The song was a huge hit and launched Collins' career into outer space. From this moment on he became a superstar and a millionaire many times over. The album still retains its magic 25 years after its release. Phil strips away the trappings of his past to indulge in the kind of music that really turns him, including the joyous freedom of soul epitomised by 'Behind The Lines'. But what turned on the public was the sense of the ordinary bloke thinking anguished thoughts aloud. There is nothing elliptical or pretentious about 'The Roof Is Leaking', a tale in which Collins muses on family misfortunes – hungry children and a waiting wife. He plays piano accompanied by a banjo and slide guitar, and sounds like he's singing in a cold, empty room. On 'Droned' Phil proves he can be as experimental as Peter Gabriel, with whom he'd just finished work on 'Intruder'.

By this time, the early Eighties, both Gabriel and Collins were at the forefront of the movement to ditch the well-worn formula of guitar based rock. Hence they utilise all manner of exotic instruments blended with synthesisers and drum machines. It says much for the skilled way in which Phil and his co-producer Hugh Padgham worked, that their 'experiments' haven't dated.

A brass section, used on 'Hand In Hand' and 'I Missed Again', lends a timeless feel to both songs. Even before the album's release, 'In The Air Tonight' got to number two in the UK charts, in February 1981. *Face Value* itself went straight to number one and went on to sell 900,000 copies in the UK alone during a 274 week run in the chart. 'I Missed Again' was Phil's first solo hit in the US where it got to number 19 while the album got to number seven. ('In The Air Tonight' was a Top Ten hit again when it was reissued in 1988). The hits, awards and royalties flowed in an unstoppable stream – and Collins was only just getting into his stride.

Hello I Must Be Going

UK issue: Virgin V2252, November 1982; US Atlantic 80035;
Re-issued Virgin CDV 2252, June 1988

THE ONLY WAY TO TOP A SMASH HIT LIKE *FACE VALUE* IS TO COME BACK with an equally impressive package of vibrant new songs. But there is one happily chosen 'cover' version here. Phil breathes new life into the Tamla Motown classic, 'You Can't Hurry Love'. Originally recorded by The Supremes in 1966, it gave Phil his first number one in the UK.

Hello I Must Be Going, produced by Phil and Hugh Padgham, is generally less neurotic in tone and certainly a lot happier than *Face Value*. Phil steams in with the aggressive 'I Don't Care Anymore', the cry of an angry man giving up on a relationship, but despite his shouts and protests it seems obvious that he still cares, even when he adds 'It Don't Matter To Me'. There is more big band power on the latter song with incredibly tight brass work from the Phoenix Horns, who arrived courtesy of Earth, Wind & Fire. Although Phil had begun to be associated with the ubiquitous drum machine, he retains his feel for a traditional kit with superb playing on the mysterious, spooky 'Thru These Walls'. Phil casually unveils his gifts as a pianist on 'Don't Let Him Steal Our Heart Away' which he sings with great tenderness, backed by sympathetic strings. He gives more generous space to the staccato Phoenix Horns stabbing through 'The West Side', a dramatic big band arrangement complete with a singularly tasteful alto sax solo.

No Jacket Required

UK issue: Virgin V2345, February 1985; US Atlantic 81420;
Re-issued Virgin CDV 2345

THE **PHOENIX HORNS MAKE THEIR PRESENCE STRONGLY FELT AGAIN ON** opening cuts 'Sussudio' and churning urn of burning funk 'Only You Know And I Know'. The sleeve note points out that 'There is no Fairlight on this record', meaning it's all real – apart from the Linn Drum machine of course, which crashes into gear on 'Don't Lose My number'.

'Sussudio' was a Top Twenty UK smash, the first hit of Spring for Phil. Actually it was his second. In the same month he'd had a hit with Philip Bailey singing 'Easy Lover'. By this time Phil was bent on world domination. A touch of The Police permeates 'Long Long Way To Go', thanks to Sting's backing vocals. He also crops up on 'Take Me Home'.

One of the finest performances is undoubtedly the perfectly formed 'One More Night', a US number one, which sold over a million. Not bad for a young lad from Chiswick. However Phil contrasts this sort of material with the hypnotic and driving 'Who Said I Would' a mix of dance rhythms and stomping brass riffs bringing out a harder vocal edge. Cascades of awards showered over 'No Jacket Required,' which stayed at number one in the UK for five weeks.

...But Seriously

UK issue: Virgin CDV 2620, November 1989; US Atlantic 82050

BUT *SERIOUSLY* **WAS THE FASTEST SELLING ALBUM IN UK HISTORY, WHEN IT** came into the chart at number one in December 1989, and stayed there for fifteen weeks. It was Collins' first album in four years, but during that time he had been furiously busy, producing for other artists (e.g. Eric Clapton's 'August') touring as the regular drummer in Clapton's band and starring in the movie *Buster*. The soundtrack album had yielded yet another huge hit, a version of the old Mindbenders song, 'A Groovy Kind Of Love'.

By 1989 Collins was a roving ambassador for rock, appearing in star packed charity shows, mixing with royalty and winning more awards than could be comfortably placed on the average suburban mantelpiece. Somehow he even managed to fit in a world tour and album with Genesis.

Eventually he got around to writing '... But Seriously', working again with Hugh Padgham. It was recorded at The Farm Studio, Surrey, and at A&M Studios in Los Angeles. Guest artists included David Crosby, Eric Clapton, Steve Winwood and Stephen Bishop, while the Phoenix Horns provided a firm foothold in funk. Their remarkable unison trumpeting invests excitement to the up tempo tracks, like 'Hang In Long Enough.' This shining, shouting piece of exuberance launches a concert-full of contrasting moods. 'Hang In Long Enough' is a blast of encouragement for those desperate to succeed and awaiting their big break.

Many of the compositions reflect aching regrets for things past, notably 'Do You Remember?' and 'Something Happened On The Way To Heaven.'

But Phil turns away from his own problems and amours to address all the troubles in the world on the heartfelt 'Colours', which points up hunger, poverty, and the lack of human rights. One of Collins' most attacking vocal performances is heard on 'I Wish It Would Rain Down', with roaring support from an inspired Eric Clapton.

The keynote song is of course 'Another Day In Paradise' about Phil's concerns with the homeless, which helped focus attention on the problem, as he was assured by many appreciative charities. A deceptively simple keyboard theme, a handclapping back beat and narrative about a tearful girl on the street with blistered feet makes its point without becoming mawkish. 'Another Day In Paradise' topped the US charts, and reached number two in the UK.

Phil at this stage in his life obviously felt many of the regrets that begin to haunt middle age, and he returns to the theme of things that should have been said, when they were most needed. This is a mood exemplified by 'All Of My Life' on which he sings: "Reaching past the goal in front of me, while what's important just slips away..."

Serious Hits... Live

Virgin PCCDX1, November 1990; US Atlantic 82157

THIS DOUBLE CD SET SERVED AS A SOUVENIR OF PHIL'S 'BUT SERIOUSLY World Tour', which featured 127 shows and visited 16 countries over a nine month period. Then he put his solo career briefly on the back burner and embarked on another major tour with Genesis, in the wake of the *We Can't Dance* album.

TRACKS: Something Happened On The Way To Heaven, Against All Odds (Take a Look at Me Now), Who Said I Would, One More Night, Don't Lose My Number, Do You Remember?, Another Day in Paradise, Separate Lives, In the Air Tonight, You Can't Hurry Love, Two Hearts, Sussudio, Groovy Kind of Love, Easy Lover, Take Me Home.

Both Sides

UK issue: Virgin 2800, November 1993

NEVER ONE TO SIT ON HIS LAURELS, PHIL CAUGHT HIS RECORD COMPANY OFF balance when he suddenly turned in this new album recorded at remarkable speed. He contributed some explanatory sleeve notes, on which he revealed he had played all the instruments on the album, which he'd made at home on a 12-track machine. Phil felt that singing the lead vocals alone without distractions meant he could give 'more heart' to his performances. They certainly sound more intimate on songs like 'Everyday', and on first impression you'd never notice that there aren't any other musicians involved, except that overall the album feels rather too comfortable and lacking in competitive spirit. Nevertheless Phil maintains in his notes: "It's the most enjoyable album I've ever made."

The title track is a look at ghetto violence, where he tries to find an explanation for the causes. On 'We're Sons Of Our Father' he despairs that the younger generation seem out of control. There is more lonely despairing introspection on songs like 'Can't Find My Way', 'Survivors' and the slow paced 'Fly So Close' which ends with the sound of rain, pain and confusion. The mood doesn't pick up much on 'There's A Place For Us' either, in which the composer seeks sanctuary with yet another loved one, promising to take her "somewhere where they don't know my face..." This could only be somewhere in Outer Mongolia.

It's altogether sadder and even more serious than ...But Seriously. Yet even the stronger, more driving songs deal with doomy subjects. 'We Wait And We Wonder' is written in response to a spate of terrorism, and the final song, 'Please Come Out Tonight', is a moving plea for companionship.

Dance Into The Light

UK issue: Face Value 630160002, October 1996

DANCE INTO THE LIGHT WAS THE FIRST COLLINS' SOLO ALBUM RELEASED since Phil announced his intention of leaving Genesis. This crucial work was upbeat in mood and contained some excellent songs. 'Light' was his brightest and best work since 'But Seriously' in 1986. Some critics suggested Peter Gabriel might have influenced the subtle 'Worldbeat' flavour. There is indeed a stylistic switch from melodic to more groove based material. However, the rhythms owe more to the Caribbean than Africa. Overall, 'Dance' proved to be a consumer friendly mix of R&B, dance-pop and sensitive ballads. The album got to number four in the UK chart and number 23 in the US.

Phil played all manner of instruments including drums, piano, bagpipes and kalimba while Brad Cole played keyboards. Nathan East from Eric Clapton's band supplied bass guitar.. After the lively title track sets the mood, 'That's What You Said' develops a strong backbeat and some effective hook lines. 'Lorenzo' has a lion's roar and strong Afro feel while 'Just Another Story is slower and more funky. 'Love Police' contains the world-weary line "I'm too tired to try" and although 'Wear My Hat' presents a merry carnival, the lyrics are a tad 'wordy'. 'It's In Your Eyes' is a better song than most and 'I Ought To Know By Now' contains the telling line "So why do you keep me hanging here with this stone around my heart?" 'Take Me Down' has a bright, fast instrumental work out while 'Same Moon' talks of packed bags and closing doors, as another relationship comes to an end. Afro rhythm impinges upon 'River So Wide' and 'No Matter Who' struts purposeful as Phil says: "Don't get lonely tonight, we can make it tonight". The final surprise is a meaningful interpretation of Bob Dylan's 'The Times They Are A Changin'", an influential anthem for all Sixties folk.

Hits

UK issue: Virgin CDV 2870, October 1998

ALTHOUGH IT SEEMED AS IF MOST THE WORLD HAD PHIL'S CASCADE OF hits still ringing in their ears, towards the end of the Nineties it seemed a timely exercise to produce a compilation that would celebrate his run of chart triumphs over the previous two decades. It was a wise move. The songs turned the public on – yet again. 'Hits' shot to number one in the UK charts and was number 18 in the US.

TRACKS INCLUDE: Another Day In Paradise, True Colours, Easy Lover, You Can't Hurry Love, Two Hearts, I Wish It Would Rain Down, Against All Odds, Something Happened On The Way To Heaven, Separate Lives, Both Sides Of The Story, One More Night, Sussudio, Dance Into The Light, A Groovy Kind Of Love, In The Air Tonight, Take Me Home.

Testify

UK issue:Face Value/East West 5046614842, November 2002;
US Warner Music/Face Value 5050466

IT WOULD BE TOO MUCH TO EXPECT PHIL COLLINS TO DEVISE YET another artistically satisfying album, having achieved so much over the previous 22 years. And so of course, he came up with... yet another great album. During the latter half of the Nineties, Phil experienced a lull in his otherwise meteoric career. He took time out to put together the Phil Collins Big Band, which enabled him to have fun and play in the style of his heroes Buddy Rich and Sonny Payne. He toured with the band in 1996 and another European and US tour followed in 1998, when they played jazz standards and original material like 'Sussudio' and 'That's All'. The band was featured live on an entertaining album *A Hot Night In Paris* (1999).

After a spell working on film soundtracks, which yielded Academy Award winning song 'You'll Be In My Heart' for the Disney movie *Tarzan* (1999), Phil returned to the fray to write and produce his first studio album since *Dance Into The Light*. Among the musicians assembled were guitarists Daryl Stuermer and Tim Pierce, Jamie Muhoberac (keyboards), and Paul Bushnel (bass). The album was given favourable reviews, one critic allowing that "Collins has aged gracefully" and citing "a welcome return to form". *Testify* was certainly created in happier circumstances. Having been through much personal trauma during the early Nineties, Collins had finally found lasting personal contentment. Secure in his marriage to new wife Orianne and rejoicing in their family life in Switzerland, Phil's lyrics reflected a growing sense of ease and thanksgiving. A warm glow spreads its light through such comforting songs as 'Come With Me' but 'Testify' is the key song. Sung sotto voce with a calming reverence Phil promises: "I will do all that I can do for you...

we will be together... I want to testify my love for you". A wonderfully subtle guitar solo by Tim Pierce matches Collins' mood. Soon the piece evolves into a blasting tumult, the drums and vocals thundering their message with gospel style passion. There is optimism as well as love in the air, evoked by the rousing opening number 'Wake Up Call' which shrills is alarm bell to a generation who risk letting a brave new world pass them by. No such danger when Phil Collins is around. "Wake up the man next to you – he's going to miss it all." The word is "This is your wake up call... young hearts be free." 'Don't Get Me Started' is a strong attack on politicians "and the lies they spread". His anger spreads to the TV and media and Phil issues a telling broadside with "I'm tired of truth being denied me. It's mine and I want it back." 'Swing Low' has a shimmering cymbal introduction that leads into a reflective piece. Collins harks back to a message from his earliest hit "about something coming in the air tonight... if it's coming let it be now". 'It's Not Too Late' has Dylan-ish vocal overtones while 'This Love This Heart' has an ethereal stillness and calm that contrasts with Collins' enduring image as the buzzing human dynamo. 'Driving Me Crazy' is an almost frantic declaration of obsessive love, while 'The Least You Can Do' commences with the anguished sound of Uillean pipes and leads into a painful plea for a past lover to "say sorry and give me back my heart". 'Can't Stop Loving You' is a driving Billy Nichols composition that was a hit for Leo Sayer in 1978. 'Thru My Eyes' offers hints about the search for happiness and meaning to life while 'You Touch My Heart' is a beautiful song that has Tim Pierce adding delicate nylon string guitar to a touching reverie about a new born child "Somehow when you smile the day seems brighter."

The Platinum Collection

Virgin, May 2004

THIS HEFTY COLLECTION FEATURES MATERIAL FROM MR. COLLINS' FIRST three blockbuster albums *Face Value*, *No Jacket Required*, and *...But Seriously*. Released during his extensive 2004 'First Final Farewell Tour' of North America, this essential triple CD set sold over 200,000 copies. Doubtless many fans had worn out their old copies of the original albums and needed replacements. There was also a new generation of record buyers, intrigued by this extraordinary library of zestful dance hits and appealing love songs, produced by an artist for whom the phrases 'prolific' and 'hard working' seem inadequate.

THE TRACKS INCLUDED: DISC 1: In The Air Tonight, This Must Be Love, Behind The Lines, Roof Is Leaking, Droned, Hand In Hand, I Missed Again, You Know What I Mean, Thunder and Lightning, I'm Not Moving, If Leaving Me Is Easy, Tomorrow Never Knows.

DISC 2: Sussudio, Only You Know And I Know, Long Long Way To Go, I Don't Wanna Know, One More Night, Don't Lose My Number, Who Said I Would, Doesn't Anybody Stay Together Anymore, Inside Out, Take Me Home, We Said Hello Goodbye.

DISC 3: Hang In Long Enough, That's Just The Way It Is, Do You Remember?, Something Happened On The Way To Heaven, Colours, I Wish It Would Rain Down, Another Day In Paradise, Heat On The Street, All Of My Life, Saturday Night And Sunday Morning, Father To Son, Find A Way Back To My Heart

Love Songs: A Compilation…
Old And New

UK issue: Virgin, September 2004 2 CD set

COLLINS THE BALLADEER IS CELEBRATED ON THIS **2 CD SET OF 25 HIT SONGS** that reflect his thoughts on all aspects of love, from yearning, passion and romance, to anger, angst and heartache. These are songs that don't just reflect the composer's personal experiences and feelings, but somehow reach out to others, who have lived, loved, won and lost. His lyrics and choice of other potent pop standards, succeed because the artists has the ability to communicate and articulate feelings in the most simple and unaffected ways. Which is of course, the secret of Phil's success – together with his trusty alarm clock ready with its early morning wake up call.

DISC 1: Tearing And Breaking, Do You Remember?, One More Night, Against All Odds, Can't Turn Back The Years, Groovy Kind Of Love, Everyday, Don't Let Him Steal Your Heart Away, Please Come Out Tonight, This Must Be Love, It's In Your Eyes, Can't Stop Loving You.

DISC 2: Testify, True Colours, You'll Be In My Heart, If Leaving Me Is Easy, I've Been Trying, I've Forgotten Everything, Somewhere, Least You Can Do, Two Hearts, Separate Lives, My Girl, Always, The Way You Look Tonight.

STEVE HACKETT

Voyage Of The Acolyte

UK issue: Charisma CAS 1111, 1975; Re-issued Charisma CASCD 1111, 1987

WITH ONE BOUND, STEVE HACKETT WAS FREE. THIS ALBUM, RELEASED two years before Steve quit the old band in 1977, was the first solo effort by a serving member and reveals strong links with Genesis, notably on the grinding 'A Tower Struck Down'. However, the album is packed with interesting arrangements and effects, and far from being a 'guitarist's' album, full of solos, the songs and moods are paramount.

Steve was fortunate in having an excellent team of musicians to support him including Phil Collins on drums and Mike Rutherford on bass and 12 string guitar. Steve's brother John Hackett is heavily featured on flute and Sally Oldfield, Mike's sister, makes a vocal contribution. Steve tries his hand at singing on 'The Hermit', a theme illustrated by an impressive cover painting by Steve's wife, Kim Poor.

The album was recorded at Kingsway Recorders, London in July 1975 and produced by Steve Hackett with John Acock.

Less bombastic than Genesis material, 'Voyage Of The Acolyte' complements rather than competes with the parent band, and with such haunting Hackett themes as 'Star Of Sirius', 'The Lovers' and 'Shadow Of The Hierophant' it remains a singularly pleasant and rewarding album.

Please Don't Touch!

UK issue: Charisma CDS 4012, 1978;
Re-issued Charisma CDSCD 4012, 1989

STEVE'S FIRST RELEASE AFTER HIS DEPARTURE FROM GENESIS IS rhythmically much stronger, while retaining many of the floating, romantic overtones inherent in Hackett's musical philosophy. This is best displayed on the opening song 'Narnia'. The vocals are imbued with greater strength by Steve Walsh, whose commanding style suits a theme inspired by C.S.Lewis' children's book (and Biblical allegory) *The Lion The Witch & The Wardrobe*. There is a touch of surrealism about 'Carry On Up The Vicarage', where Hackett sings courtesy of speeded up and slowed down tapes. Every track has something of interest, whether it's a peculiar lyric, strange sound effect, or simply an intriguing melody. It's a circus of musical attractions, given rhythmic impetus by Chester Thompson making a guest appearance on drums. On 'Kim' Steve plays a brief acoustic classical guitar interlude, while brother John adds fragile flute. American singer Richie Havens makes am unexpected appearance on the Beatle-y 'How Can I?', while Randy Crawford offers a superb vocal on the moving string-laden ballad 'Hoping Love Will Last'.

Packed with goodies, *Please Don't Touch* is a musical cornucopia of ideas. Hackett has produced a steady stream of albums over the years, worth investigating, including *Spectral Mornings* (Charisma CDS 4017, 1979), *Defector* (Charisma CDS 4018, 1980), *Cured* (Charisma CDS 4021, 1981), *Till We Have Faces* (Lamborghini CDLMG 4000,1984), *Momentum* (1988) and *Highly Strung* (Virgin HAKCD 1, 1989).

Subsequent albums include *Unauthorised Biography* (1992), *Time Lapse* (1992), *Guitar Noir* (1993), *There Are Many Sides To The Night* (1994), *Blues With A Feeling* (1994), *Watcher Of The Skies – Genesis Revisited* (1996), *Steve Hackett & Friends* (1996), *A Midsummer Night's Dream* (1997), *The Tokyo Tapes* (1998), *Darktown* (1999), *Sketches Of Satie* (2000), *Guitar Classique* (2001), and *To Watch The Storms* (2003). All of them are worth investigating and reflect Hackett's range of influences from blues, classical and folk to jazz, rock and New Age music.

TONY BANKS

A Curious Feeling

UK issue: Charisma CAS 1148, 1979; Re-issue CASCD 1148, 1988

TONY BANKS HAS BEEN THE DRIVING FORCE BEHIND GENESIS SINCE ITS inception. A classically trained musician, he has released a succession of well made solo albums over the years, most reflecting his desire to create commercially acceptable rock/pop music rather than celebrate his skills as a virtuoso keyboard player. This has given him the opportunity to work with different vocalists and musicians outside of the Genesis sphere, including Scots singer Fish, formerly front man of the group Marillion. Tony has been at pains to produce albums that have a range of carefully crafted songs that are not just platforms for extended instrumental work. His first album *A Curious Feeling* did well on release, entering the UK chart at 21 in November 1979. Genesis drummer Chester Thompson backs Tony's keyboard work here and the lyrics are delivered by Kim Beacon. The album was produced by David Hentschel and Tony Banks, and recorded at Polar Music Studios, Stockholm. Among the most appealing tracks are 'From The Undertow', 'Lucky Me', 'A Curious Feeling' and 'In The Dark'. 'For A While' was issued as a single but without chart success.

The Fugitive

UK issue: Virgin TBCD 1, 1983

A SELECTION OF ORIGINAL SONGS THAT FEATURE TONY BANKS IN A NEW role as lead vocalist. He gives voice to such songs as 'This Is Love', 'Man Of Spells', 'And The Wheels Keep Turning' and 'Say You'll Never Leave Me'. A drum machine is employed on the track 'Thirty Threes' to lend a contemporary feel, but Tony lacks the vocal punch necessary to compete with his more heavy weight rivals.

It seemed he could not find the right niche between his classical leanings and pop aspirations but it wasn't for the lack of trying.

Banks Statement

UK issue: Virgin CDV 2600 1989

A VAST IMPROVEMENT ON 'THE FUGITIVE' THANKS TO THE ADDITION OF singer Alistair Gordon, and the powerful Phantom Horns who ride into the opening cut 'Throwback' with all trumpets blowing. There are some interesting ideas, like the heavy breathing that permeates 'I'll Be Waiting' which may have been the idea of co-producer Steve Hillage.

Generally the music has more in common with the late Eighties' pop chart than anything Hillage and Banks created in the Prog rock Seventies. One of strongest items is 'Queen Of Darkness', which gets up a head of steam, while Jayney Klimek adds pleasant backing vocals to the pretty 'That Night'. The lyrical ideas are not exactly inspired – viz. "... who knows what tomorrow may bring..." and ennui sets in rapidly on 'The Border'. The composer perks up on 'Big Man' where he makes effective use of synth in Stevie Wonder 'Superstition' style.

Still

UK issue: Virgin V/CDV 2568, 1992

TONY BANKS' MOST AMBITIOUS PROJECT SINCE *BANKS STATEMENT*, *STILL* features pop star Nick Kershaw (vocals) as well as old friend Fish and the top session men of the day, including Sting's regular drummer Vinnie Colaiuta. Daryl Stuermer (guitar), Pino Palladino (bass) and Graham Broad (drums) complete a strong team. Among the ten tracks are 'Red Day On Blue Street', 'Angel Face', 'The Gift', 'Still It Takes Me By Surprise', 'Here for An Hour', 'I Wanna Change The Score', 'Water Out Of Wine', 'Another Murder Of A Day', 'Back To Back' and 'The Final Curtain'. Critics were kinder to this album than some of Tony's previous efforts, but it still failed to ignite the charts.

In the future he would move away from writing pop material and instead concentrated on composing classical themes. This resulted in his album Seven (Naxos) released in 2004 on which the London Philharmonic Orchestra performed his 'Suite For Orchestra'. Among the seven pieces were 'Spring Tide', 'Black Down', 'The Gateway', 'The Ram', 'Earthlight', 'Neap Tide' and 'The Spirit Of Gravity'.

MIKE RUTHERFORD

Small Creep's Day

UK issue: Charisma CAS 1149; Re-issue Charisma CASCD 1149, June 1989

MIKE, THE UNSUNG HERO OF GENESIS, MAKES A FINE DÉBUT THAT did encouragingly well on first release, when it got to number 13 in the UK chart in March 1980. With a live feel, plenty of real drums and guitars, tracks like 'Working In Line' could easily pass for mid-Seventies Genesis. Side one is devoted to the diary of a Mr. Nobody, one 'Smallcreep' who goes about his daily tasks at the factory, ensnared in a nine to five routine, and a boring life style alleviated by dreams of love. It's a simple theme, inspired by the book *Smallcreep's Day*, by Peter Currell Brown.

Rutherford's solo efforts show a strong sense of direction and are assured and imaginative. Drummer Simon Phillips, with Anthony Phillips on guitar, ably assists Mike on the project. Noel McCalla imbues the songs with his authorative vocal style. Rutherford, who wrote all the material, plays guitars and basses.

Acting Very Strange

UK issue: WEA K99249, September 1982

THE DEFT HAND OF RUTHERFORD IS REVEALED TO EVEN BETTER ADVANTAGE on a second solo album, which develops a character further away from early Genesis, although perhaps closer in spirit to the subsequent sound of *Invisible Touch*. The title track has welcome good humour and seems influenced by The Jam's energy and the madness of Madness. Mike takes the lead vocals with surprisingly 'street cred' overtones. Mike's Genesis colleague, Daryl Stuermer plays lead guitar, and rhythmic pulse is provided Stewart Copeland of The Police. Mike produced the entire album himself at The Farm, Surrey, and the result remains a varied and entertaining selection of vibrant songs, like 'A Day To Remember' and 'Maxine' powered with a heavy back beat. There's even a Police-style touch of reggae on 'Halfway There'. 'Who's Fooling Who' drives like Genesis with a brass section. One of the most telling songs is 'Couldn't Get Arrested', with the chanted line "You kept on investing all you had... had this gift no one else could see it... you knew you had it, long before they found it!" It is the song of the frustrated songwriter who finally makes good..

Mike & The Mechanics

UK issue: WEA 252 4961, 1985

A **JOYOUS RESULT FOR MIKE RUTHERFORD, WHOSE ANGUISHED CRY OF** 'Couldn't Get Arrested' on *Acting Very Strange*, is answered with the heart-warming success of this album. The Mechanics were a fine new band that featured gifted singers Paul Carrack (ex-Ace and Squeeze), and Paul Young (from Manchester's Sad Café). With Peter Van Hooke on drums and Mike returning to guitars and bass, the Mechanics revealed a happy blend of expertise and enthusiasm. Most of the material on this debut album was written by Mike in collaboration with Christopher Neil and B.A. Robertson.

Stand out songs include the smash hits 'Silent Running' and 'All I Need Is A Miracle'. The former was from the film *On Dangerous Ground* and was a number six hit in America and reached 21 in the UK in February 1986. 'All I Need Is A Miracle', one of the great pop songs of the age, went to number five in the States in June, but mysteriously failed to chart higher than 53 in the UK. Curiously enough one of the Mechanics' songs here, 'Par Avion', includes the line "Another day in paradise" and is sung over a gentle drum machine rhythm. The third single from the album 'Taken In' was also a chart hit in the US. Packed with mature, well crafted songs like the swinging 'I Get The Feeling' this album has a happier feel than any other produced by solo Genesis men.

The Living Years

UK release: WEA 256004 2, 1988

Y **OUNG FANS OF MIKE & THE MECHANICS HAD NO IDEA THAT 'MIKE'** was connected with a legendary rock band their parents listened to in the Seventies. Some TV interviewers didn't make the connection either, and Mike would sit and smile innocently and tell them what it was like to be part of a successful new band. Key song on this warmly welcomed second album is title track 'The Living Years', with a touching lyric about a father and son relationship, written by Rutherford and

B.A.Robertson. The song got to number two in the UK and topped the US charts in January 1989, while the album peaked at number two in the UK.

Word Of Mouth

UK release: Virgin CDV 2662, May 1991

A **SUPERB COLLECTION OF SONGS GRACED BY PENETRATING VOCALS FROM** Paul Carrack and Paul Young, and invigorated by Christopher Neil and Mike Rutherford's expert production. 'Get Up' has an attacking keyboard pattern that paves the way for positive lyrics that urge listeners to "get up and do something with your life." It's a theme that Phil Collins would take up again with 'Wake Up Call' on his *Testify* album some years later. It's also a song for all parents with offspring prone to idle in a bed all day. The title track has an irresistible hook line, and performances like 'A Time And Place' easily match anything produced by colleagues Collins or Gabriel.

Beggar On A Beach Of Gold

UK issue: Virgin CV 2772, February 1995

R **ICH IN INTELLIGENT, CARING LYRICS AND STRONG MELODIES, THE MECHANICS'** 1995 hot property is low on introspective angst but strong on optimism. "Don't look back, don't give up" is the message, for example, on the compulsive 'Another Cup Of Coffee'. Venturing away from their own songs, The Mechanics pay tribute to Smokey Robinson with a thoughtful version of 'You Really Got A Hold On Me' which The Beatles covered on their second album, and offer a splendid cover of Stevie Wonder's 'I Believe (When I Fall In Love It Will Be Forever)'.

But it's the original material that gives this album its strength, with unusual concepts like 'The Ghost Of Sex And You' and 'Web Of Lies'. Paul Young's vocal flair is backed with extra blues power courtesy of guest guitarist Clem Clempson. 'Plain And Simple' rocks with a menacing power that harks back to Free. The renewed success of the band has undoubtedly been heart-warming for Mike Rutherford, who like Collins and Gabriel has been able to enjoy more than one career during a lifetime of achievement.

Rewired

Original UK issue: Virgin EMI CDV2984, released 2004

MIKE **RUTHERFORD** **AND** **CO-WRITER** **AND** **LEAD** **SINGER** Paul Carrack were reunited for the band's first studio album in five years and the first since the sudden death of former Mechanics singer Paul Young in July 2000, aged 53. The critically acclaimed album was two years in the making and features two instrumental tracks 'Rewind' and 'Underscore'. The songs included 'One Left Standing', 'If I Were You', 'Perfect Child', 'I Don't Want It All', 'How Can I', 'Falling' and 'Somewhere Along The Line'. A thoroughly modern album with techno and funk overtones it was accompanied by a limited edition DVD (CDVX 2984). Mike & The Mechanics toured Europe in support of the release in the summer of 2004.

Index

(Genesis Songs Only)